End of Days

The Apocalyptic Writings

The Apocalypse of Abraham,
The Apocalypse of Thomas, or The Revelation of Thomas
4 Ezra, also referred to as 2 Esdras or the Apocalypse of Ezra
2 Baruch, also known as the Syriac Apocalypse of Baruch

Compiled by Joseph B. Lumpkin

With editing assistance from Joyce Dujardin

Joseph B. Lumpkin

END OF DAYS - The Apocalyptic Writings

Copyright © 2007 Joseph Lumpkin
All rights reserved.

Printed in the United States of America. No section (piece) of this book may be used or reproduced in any manner whatsoever without written permission except in the case of brief quotations embodied in critical articles and reviews.
All people and facts in this book are fictions. Any resemblance to real people or facts is coincidental.

Fifth Estate Publishers,
Post Office Box 116, Blountsville, AL 35031.

First Printing 2007
Cover are by
Printed on acid-free paper
Library of Congress Control No: 2007904049
ISBN: 1-933580-38-0

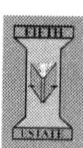

Fifth Estate
2007

END of DAYS - The Apocalyptic Writings

Joseph B. Lumpkin

Introduction

Is mankind headed for destruction? How will it all end? When will it happen? What is man's destiny? Will we die by our own hand or by the hand of God?

For thousands of years the questions have been the same. Millions of souls have searched for the answers to no avail; nevertheless, some believed they knew. We call them prophets. They saw the end of our world and they believed their visions were true. Are we to believe their God-given insights into the End Of Days?

Perhaps God did pull back the curtain that blinds man to his future. Maybe these writers did see the end and how it would come upon us.

The prophets of doom revealed a scenario of global cataclysm. They tell the story of rulers bankrupting nations to fund tremendous wars. They tell of weather gone awry; of ice and snow, rain and floods, hurricanes and earthquakes where seldom they occurred. They tell us of what is happening all around us today.

Most scholars agree that many of the apocalyptic texts written between 70 and 200 A.D. were produced out of a national dismay and confusion following the destruction of the temple of the Jews in Israel in 70 A.D. The texts are attempts of a people, who believed themselves to be God's chosen, to explain why pagans were allowed by the God of the Jews to overthrow the way of worship, and of life of His chosen ones. Other apocalyptic books were written to explain and expand various biblical ideas linked to judgment and the end of days. The date, background, and purpose of each text will be discussed in more detail later.

The apocalyptic literature presented here allows us a rare glimpse into the ancient mindset and visions of how mankind may end. Most writings of this kind took place between 200 B.C. and 200 A.D, although a few were later and dated to the third century. The common thread was the moral and spiritual decline of man leading to his destruction. One could argue that the annihilation of the human race was to be brought about by our own hands due to our evil and sinful ways; however, it is the power unleashed by the wrath of God that gives way to the cleansing of the earth as all evil is destroyed and divine order is re-established. Only those who followed God and kept his laws would be spared.

Books written by those claiming to be Abraham, Thomas, Ezra, Baruch, and other giants of faith come down to us in ancient scrolls proclaiming the exact sequence of events leading to mankind's termination. Every society possesses apocalyptic texts. Every race and every nation carries in its literature and religion the implicit reiterating and unrelenting question; is the end near? The answer…yes, it is and here are its signs.

Presented in this book are four great apocalyptic works. "The Apocalypse of Abraham," "The Apocalypse Of Thomas" which is also called "The Revelation of Thomas," 2 Baruch, which is also known as the Syriac Apocalypse of Baruch, and 4 Ezra, sometimes also referred to as 2 Esdras or the Apocalypse of Ezra.

These books represent the greatest among the apocalyptic writings of the era. Each gives its own unique insights into the End Of Days and yet, they all proclaim the same message; Follow God, turn from evil, or be destroyed.

The Apocalypse of Abraham

"The Apocalypse of Abraham" is part of a body of writings called "Abrahamic Writings," which flourished around and just after the time of Christ.

The manuscript dates from A.D. 80-170 with most scholars placing it between 80 and 100 A.D. The original text was written in a Semitic language, however it has survived only in Old Slavonic renditions.

Many of the Jewish non-canonical and extra-biblical materials that circulated in the Slavic lands came from Byzantium. They greatly influenced the development of Slavic literature. Non-canonical books brought from Byzantium were translated and became sections (pieces) of various Slavonic traditions. The Eastern Orthodox church nurtured an environment in which the apocryphal texts were encouraged toward the view of providing additional information as a secondary source to the canonical mainstream texts. Pseudepigraphical (certain writings other than the canonical books and the Apocrypha, professing to be Biblical in character) texts attributed to Adam, Enoch, Noah, Jacob, Abraham, Moses, and other patriarchs survived in this environment and were incorporated in hagiographical (the writing and critical study of the lives of the saints) and historical volumes.

An English translation of "The Apocalypse of Abraham" was produced by G. H. Box and J. I. Landsman in 1918 (The Apocalypse of Abraham, London: Society for Promoting Christian Knowledge) but that translation does not read well for the modern English audience. Thus arises the need to have the Box and other mainstream translations combined and updated into a more readable and accessible mode for today's reader.

It should be noted here that there are two versions of the "Apocalypse of Abraham," a long and a short version. The text in the book before you contains a combination of these two versions. When the two versions agree, which was more often than not the case, the clearest and best wording was chosen to express both in a single phrase.

When there were variations in meaning, alternate translations are shown in parentheses. When one version covered information not contained in the other translation, the additional lines were added, making this book the most complete body of information available as a single text.

"The Apocalypse of Abraham" is written in an haggadic midrash tradition. (Haggadic - embracing the interpretation of the non-legal portions of the Hebrew Bible. These midrashim are sometimes referred to as *haggadah*, a term that refers to all non-legal discourse in classical rabbinic literature). (Midrash – a Hebrew word referring to a method of exegesis of a Biblical text and teachings in the form of legal or exegetical commentaries on the Jewish Bible).

As with much of the Haaadic literature, the writings are an expansion and detailed explanation of existent biblical texts. That is to say, the writer took a section of an Old Testament canonical text and expanded it into a larger, more detailed story in order to explain in further detail the moral and religious implications of the original text.

Apocalyptic writings abound in the same time frame in the first century. It is thought they were spurred into creative existence by the utter destruction of the Jewish Temple in 70 A.D. and the attempted annihilation of Christians, many of whom were converted Jews, at the same time.

"The Apocalypse of Abraham" is based on Genesis 15:9-17 and concludes with the apocalypse. The book is of Jewish origin with features which might suggest that it had its beginning in the Essene community. This is seen clearly in the references to the "Elect One," a term that also appears in the Lost Book Of Enoch." (See "The Lost Book Of Enoch" by Joseph Lumpkin.)

Approximately one-third of the "Apocalypse of Abraham" contains an account of Abraham's conversion from polytheism to henotheism. Whereas polytheism believes in and worships many gods, each according to his or her dominion and special power; monotheism is the belief in one god; and henotheism focuses on one god but does not deny the existence of the other gods. The Amarna period of Egyptian history is an example a society that held to the henotheistic belief system.

The apocalyptic section of the Abraham text begins with the search for the God that made all things and the rejection of god's (idols) made by men. He (Abraham) reasons that if man made the gods with his own hands that man must therefore be greater than the gods he made.

Abraham's prayers are answered and he is told how to sacrifice to God. The preparation and sacrifice follows the biblical account, except that instead of birds of prey appearing and consuming the sacrifice, it is Azazel who does so. The angel Jaoel (Iaoel or Joel), guides Abraham into heaven and teaches him a song that is to be sung only on that realm or sphere of heaven.

While in heaven, Abraham sees a vision of the sin and degradation of his own progeny. As their sin increases, God withdraws his protection and the great temple is overrun by "heathen nations" and the progeny is killed and enslaved.

The five main characters in the book are El (God), Jaoel, Azazel, Abraham, and a powerful figure simply known as "The Man." There are also minor characters such as Abraham's father and merchants who travel in the area in which Abraham lived.

We learn in the first chapter of the Apocalypse of Abraham that Abraham is the son of Terah and the brother of Nahor.

Joseph B. Lumpkin

Chapter 1

1. I was standing guard one day over the gods of my father Terah and my brother Nahor...

We also know Abraham's family were polytheists who worshipped idols that their father made. We learn that Terah sold his idols to others as well. Abraham is depicted as a precocious and sassy youth who questions things taken for granted by others.

He asked a question that seems most insightful for its time; If you carve an idol to worship as a god, does not that make you greater than the god you made? If that is true, why worship that which is lesser? This simple question puts him on the path of searching for the God who made all things including man.

Jaoel is the angel assigned to guide Abraham on his search. Jaoel takes him to heaven and leads him into visions, instructing him along the way.

Since Jaoel is allowed to come and go from the seventh heaven, we must assume him to be an angel of very high rank, though not found mentioned by this name elsewhere.

The name Jaoel consists of two parts, Jah and El both names of God in the Old Testament. Jaoel shows and explains a universal duality.

The duality of the universe is seen in the "right handed" and "left handed" principle. The Lord Himself used this principle when speaking of the 'sheep and the goats" in Matthew 25.

Here in the Abrahamic writings there are people coming out of a temple on the left side and on the right side. The deities in the story are the God El, who in this writing assumes the name of Azazel, a name that appears a great deal in the Books of Enoch, and is used in the Old Testament in the account of the Day of Atonement, where one goat is slain in the Tabernacle, whilst the other is set free, and the Hebrew text reads it is "for Azazel."

Azazel is portrayed as an unclean bird which came down upon the sacrifice Abraham, the Biblical patriarch, prepared. This is in reference to Genesis 15:11 Birds of prey came down upon the carcasses, and Abram drove them away.

Azazel is also associated with Hell. Abraham tells Azazel he will burn in hell and be in the underworld or Hades.

Azazel appears four times in Old Testament: Leviticus 16 :8, 10, and 26, where the ritual for the Day of Atonement is described. After the priest has made atonement for himself, he is to take two goats on behalf of Israel. One is to be a sacrifice to the Lord, the other is to be the 'scape goat,' which is the goat for Azazel.

This word has been understood to mean the "goat that departs," considering it to be derived from two Hebrew words: "ez" (goat) and "azal" (turn off). It is also associated with the Arabic word, "azala" (banish), or (remove), It has been rendered "for entire removal." Refer to Leviticus 16:22. However, in I Chronicles 5:8, the father of Bela, a Reubenite, is named "Azaz," which means strong.

This name comes from the Hebrew verb "azaz", a which means "to be strong." Azazel is also seen as an evil spirit in Enoch 8:1; 10:4; II Chroncicles 11:15; Isaiah 34:14; and Revelations 18:2. In this way Azazel can be seen as the opponent or antithesis to the Lord and a precursor to Satan.

The figure of "The Man" is rather ambiguous. He is not fully messianic, yet he is endowed with power from God.

He may have come from the Essene idea of the Teacher of Righteousness and his connection with the coming, expected messiah.

Another explanation of the figure may come from an early Christian idea originating in a Judeo-Christian sect, which saw Jesus as precursor of the real and awaited Messiah, or it may simply be a Jewish text being badly interpreted and biased by an early Christian editor.

The evolution of El and his origin has drawn debate and acrimony since the beginning of theological study.

The people of Aramean and Canaanite origin seem to have contributed to the religion of El. Both religions place El as the highest god of a pantheon. Yet, because there is a pantheon of gods there is polytheism.

The clearest example of this adoption of the Israelite Elism comes from Deuteronomy 32 and related texts. El rules over his sons, and assigns each of them a people or tribe to govern. Here, to our surprise, we find Yahweh (the Lord) portrayed as one of El Elyon's divine sons.

Psalm 29 shows Yahweh as one of the sons of El, but a powerful god who is less subordinate than the others and more like an elder son.

Psalm 29 introduces the Canaanite cosmology which was more simple and familial; El being the father image and king.

We find within the Israelite religion two variations of the same high god. These different versions of Elism (the belief in a god called El) show that this god was variously worshipped depending upon location. Locations north of Palestine would have brought the worship of Yahweh in contact with Canaanite religion and that may explain its distinctly Canaanite quality.

Continuing the relationship between El and his sons, Psalm 82 has El stripping all his sons of authority and condemning them to mortality.

From this viewpoint, the Aramean god, El, seems to be related Canaanite mythology. Both likely descended from a Mesopotamian religion.

Yet now, after being failed and disappointed by all others gods, whom we presume are his sons, El is forced to rule alone. Now we have the pathway set between polytheism and monotheism.

This last steps between the idea of a ruling court of gods and the singular god, El, can be seen clearly in the following translation and study by John Gray, Near Eastern Mythology:

> "God has taken His place in the assembly of the gods (lit. 'sons of El"),
> He declares His judgment among the gods: "
> How long will you give crooked judgment,
> and favor the wicked?
> You ought to sustain the case of the weak and the orphan;
> You ought to vindicate the destitute and down-trodden
> You ought to rescue the weak and the poor,
> To deliver them from the power of the wicked
> You (Hebrew "they") walk in darkness
> While all earth's foundations are giving away.
> I declare "Gods you may be,
> Sons of the Most high, all of you;
> Yet you will die as men,
> You will fall as one of the bright ones."
>   Psalm 82:1-7

"In the final line we read sharim for sarim ("princes"), from which it is indistinguishable in the Hebrew manuscripts, and find another reference to the fall of Athtar, the bright Venus star in Isaiah 14:12 ff and in the myth of Baal." (John Gray, <u>Near Eastern Mythology</u>)

Now, having introduced the cast of characters and set the historical and theological stage, let us proceed to the "Apocalypse of Abraham."

Joseph B. Lumpkin

The Apocalypse of Abraham

Chapter 1

1. I was standing guard one day over the gods of my father Terah and my brother Nahor.

2. While I was testing them to find out which god was really the strongest and I was completing the services, I, Abraham, received my chance.

3. My father Terah was sacrificing to his gods of wood, stone, gold, silver, copper, and of iron and I entered their temple for the service, and found a god named Marumath, carved from stone, which had fallen at the feet of the iron god, Nakhin.

4. At that point my heart was perplexed (troubled) and I thought that I could not put it back in its place by myself because of its weight, since it was made of large stones.

5. So, I went and told my father, and he came in with me. When we both lifted it to put it in its place, its head fell off while I was holding it by its head.

6. Then when my father saw that the head of his god Marumath had fallen.

7. He yelled at me, saying, "Abraham!"

8. And I said, "Here I am!" And he told me to bring me the axes and chisels from the house. So, I brought them to him from the house.

9. Then he cut another Marumath without a head from another stone. He then smashed the head that had fallen off Marumath. He then crushed the rest of that (broken) Marumath.

Chapter 2

1. He created five more gods and gave them to me. He ordered me to sell them outside on the road to town.

2. I saddled my father's ass and loaded the gods on it and went out on the highway to sell them.

3. The merchants from Phandana of Syria were coming with their camels, on their way to Egypt to buy kokonil from the Nile.

4. I questioned them and they answered me. I walked along with them and talked with them. Then, one of their camels screamed and the ass was frightened and fled, throwing off the gods. Three of them were broken and two remained intact.

5. Then the Syrians saw that I had gods, they said to me: "Why did you not tell us that you had gods? We would have bought them before the ass. heard the camel's cry. You would had lost nothing."

6. Then they said, "Give us the gods that remain and we will give you a suitable price."

7. I considered this and grieved. But they paid both for the smashed gods and the gods which remained. I had been worried how I would bring payment to my father.

8. I threw the three broken gods into the water of the river Gur, which was in this place. And they sank deeply into the river Gur and were not seen again.

Chapter 3

1. As I was still walking on the road, my heart was disturbed and my mind was distracted.

2. I thought, "What is this deed of inequality my father is doing?

3. Is it not he who is god because his gods come into being through his sculpting, planning, and his skill (workmanship)?

4. They ought to honor my father because the gods are his work. What reward does my father received for his works?

5. Marumath fell and could not stand up in his (own) sanctuary, and could not I lift him myself until my father came and we stood him up (together). Even then we were not able to do it and his head fell off of him.

7. Then he put another stone on it from another god, which he (my father) had made without a head. The other five gods which got smashed when they fell from the ass could not save themselves. They did not harm the ass (to avenge themselves) because it smashed them. Nor did their broken pieces come up out of the river.

8. And I thought to myself, "If this is so, how can my father's god Marumath, which has the head of one stone and is made from another stone, save a man, or hear a man's prayer, or grant him any gift?"

Chapter 4

1. Thinking this way, I came to my father's house. I watered the ass and fed the ass with hay. I took out the silver and placed it in my father Terah's hand.

2. And when he saw it, he was happy, and he said, "You are blessed, Abraham, by the god of my gods, since you have brought me the price for the gods, so that my labor was not empty (for nothing)."

3. I answered and said to him, "Listen, father Terah! In you is the blessing of your gods, because you are the god of them, since you created them because their blessing is their hell and their power is empty.

4. They did not help themselves; how then can they help you or bless me?

5. I did well for you in this transaction, because through my good sense I brought you the silver for the broken gods."

6. When he heard what I had to say he became violently angry with me, since I had spoken words harshly contrary to his gods.

Chapter 5

1. Having thought about my father's anger, I left.
2. And afterward when I had left, he called me saying, "Abraham!" I answered, "Here I am!"
3. He said, " Gather these wood chips. I was making gods from fir before you came.
4. I will use the chips to cook food when I prepared my midday meal."
5. Then, when I was picking up the wooden chips, I found a small god among them which would fit in my left hand.
6. On its forehead was written: god Barisat. Then, I put the chips on the fire in to prepare food for my father, and went out to ask him about the food, I put Barisat near the kindling for the fire.
7. I spoke to him as if to threaten him. I said, "Barisat, watch that the fire does not go out before I come back!
8. If the fire goes out, blow on it so it flares up." I went out and said nothing of this to anyone.
9. When I returned I found Barisat fallen on his back. His feet were enveloped by fire and burning fiercely.
10. When I saw it, I laughed and I said to myself, "Barisat, truly you know how to light a fire and cook food!"
11. Then, while saying this in my laughter, I saw that he had burned up slowly with fire and turned to ashes.
12. I carried the food to my father to eat.
13. I gave him wine and milk, and he drank and he enjoyed himself and he thanked and spoke praise to Marumath his god.

14. Then I said to him, "Father Terah, do not bless Marumath your god, do not praise him!

15 Instead, praise your god Barisat, because he loved you enough that he threw himself into the fire in order to cook your food."

16. Then my father said to me said, "Where is he now?" And I said, "He has burned in the flames of the fire and become dust." And he said, "Great is the power of Barisat! I will make another today, and tomorrow he will prepare my food."

Chapter 6

1. When I, Abraham, heard these words from my father, I laughed to myself and I groaned from the disgust and anger in my heart.

2. I said, "How can a piece of a body made (by Terah) help my father, Terah?

3. How can he have enslaved his body to his soul (will or desire), and allowed his soul (will or desire) to be enslaved by a spirit (not his spirit but "a" spirit), when the spirit is stupid and ignorant?"

4. And I said, "It is only proper to withstand this evil that I may compel my mind toward purity. I will lay my thoughts out before him clearly.

5. " I answered and said, "Father Terah, no matter which of these gods you praise, your thoughts err.

6. Don't you see that the gods of my brother Nahor which stand in the holy sanctuary are more worthy than yours?

7. Look! Zouchaios, my brother Nahor's god is more worthy than your god Marumath because he is made of gold, which is valued by man.

8. And if Zouchaios grows old with time, he will be remolded, whereas, if Marumath deteriorates or is broken, he will not be renewed, because he is made of stone.

9. What about Ioav, the other god who stands with Zouchaios? He is also more worthy than the god Barisat.

10. He, Ioay, is carved from wood and then forged from silver; because he too is made of something that is given with love (comparison), and is valued by man according to their outward experience.

11. But Barisat, your god, is rooted in the earth. When he was large (great) it is a wonder because he had branches and flowers and was worth praise when he was still not carved.

12. But then you shaped him with an axe and you created (him as) a god by your skill.

13. Look! He has already dried up.

14. His substance (fruit/fatness) has perished.

15. From the height he has fallen to the earth.

16. He descended from greatness to a lowly state, and his face and appearance has wasted (withered) away.

17. He was burned up by the fire and he turned into ashes and disappeared.

18. Then you say, "Let me make another and tomorrow he will prepare my food for me." He was destroyed and no power (strength) was left in him (because of or to prevent) his own destruction.

Chapter 7

1. This I say: Fire is more valuable in the formation of things because even the untamable things are subdued in (by) it, and it laughs at those things which are destroyed easily by its burning.

3. But neither is it worthy (valuable), because it is subject to the water.

4. But water is more worthy (venerable/powerful) than fire because water overcomes fire and sweetens the earth with fruit.

5. But I would not call water a god either because water is taken under the earth and water is subject to the earth.

6. I will not call earth a goddess either because it is dried by the sun and was made for man for his work.

7. I think the sun is more worthy among the gods, because with its rays it illuminates the entire universe and all the air.

8. But I will would not place the sun among the gods because there are those who obscure his course. They are the moon and the clouds.

9. I will not call the moon or the stars gods, because at times during the night they also dim their light.

10. Listen, Terah my father, I will seek the God who created all the other gods we have thought exist.

11. I seek who or what is it that made the heavens red and the sun golden and who has given light to the moon and the stars and who has dried the earth in the midst of the many waters. I will seek who it is that has set you yourself among the things and who has sought me out in the of my thoughts of questioning.

12. God will reveal himself by himself to us!"

Chapter 8

1. Then, I was thinking about my father Terah being in the court of my house when the voice of the Mighty One came down from the heavens in a stream of fire and it called to me saying, "Abraham, Abraham!"

2. And I said, "Here I am."

3. Then he said, "You are searching in the wisdom of your heart for the God of gods, the Creator? I am he.

4. Get out from Terah, your father, and go away from the house, that you too may not be killed because of the sins of your father's house."

5. Then, as I went out and I was not outside the entrance of the court yet, the sound of a tremendous thunder came and burned him and his house and everything in his house to the ground for a space of forty cubits.

Chapter 9

1. Then a voice spoke to me twice: "Abraham, Abraham!"

2 I said, "Here I am!" And He said, "Look! It is I, fear not for I am with you because I AM before the ages, I am the Mighty God who created the first light of the world. I am your protection (shield) and your helper."

3. He continued and said, "Behold, it is I, Fear not because I am Before the World Was, I Am Mighty, the God who has created all, I am the light of the age.

4. I am your protector and your helper.

5. Go, get me a three-year-old heifer, a three-year-old female goat, a three-year-old ram, a turtledove, and a pigeon.

6. Go, take me a young heifer of three years, and a female goat of three years, and a ram of three years, a turtledove and a pigeon, and bring me a pure sacrifice.

7. In this sacrifice I will lay before (make known to) you the ages to come, and tell you what is in store, and you will see great things which you have not seen before.

8. I will tell you things kept guarded and you will see great things which you have not seen, because you desired me and searched for me, and so I called you my beloved.

9. But for forty days abstain from every kind of food cooked by fire, and from drinking because you have loved to search me out, and I have named you "my friend."

10 And also abstain from anointing yourself with oil for forty days, and then give me the sacrifice which I have commanded you, in a place which I will show you high on a mountain, and there I will reveal to you the ages which have been created and established by my word.

11. (And there I will show you the things which were made in the ages and by my word that affirmed and created, and renewed.) I will make known to you what will come to pass for them who have done evil and for those who have done righteousness (just deeds) in the generations of men."

Chapter 10

1. Then, I heard the voice telling me such things.
2. And I heard the voice of Him who spoke these words to me, and I looked around (for Him).
3. I found I could not breathe, and fear seized my spirit. My soul seemed to leave me and I fell down like a stone, like a dead man falls to the earth, and I had no strength to stand.
4. I was laying with my face down to the earth when I heard the voice of the Holy One speaking, "Go, Jaoel, and by the power of my ineffable name raise up man, that man over there and strengthen him , so that he recovers from his trembling.
5. Consecrate this man for me and strengthen him against his trembling."
6. The angel he sent to me in the likeness of a man came, and he took me by my right (hand) and set me up upon my feet and said to me, "Stand up Abraham, friend of God who loves you. Do not let your trembling seize you! For look! I have been sent to you to strengthen you and bless you in the name of God, who loves you. He is the Creator of the heaven and the Earth. Do not fear but and run to Him.
7. I am called Jaoel by Him who gives life to those who exist with me on the seventh level of heaven. It is done by the power of the goodness of the ineffable name that is dwelling in me.
8. I am the one who has been given (the authority) to restrain the threats and attacks of the Living One's Cherubim against one another, and to teach those who have Him within them, the song of the seventh hour of the night

of man, according to His commandment. (I teach those who carry the song through man's night of the seventh hour.)

9. I am the one who ordered your father's house to be burned with him because he honored the dead (gods).

10. I am given authority to restrain the Leviathan (serpent/reptiles) because every attack and menace of every Leviathan (serpent/reptile) are subject to me.

11. I am he who has been given power to loosen Hades, and destroy him who watches over the dead.

12. I have been sent to bless you and your land now, for the Eternal One whom you have invoked has prepared for you. For your sake I have ventured my way upon earth.

13. Stand up, Abraham, go boldly, be very joyful and rejoice. And I (also rejoice) with you because you are venerable and I am with you! For everlasting honor has been prepared for you by the Eternal One.

14. Go, and do the sacrifices commanded. For I, and with me Michael, blesses you forever.

15. I have been commanded to be with you, and with the generations that will spring from you, Be of good cheer and go!"

Chapter 11

1.. And I stood up and saw him who had grasped me by the right hand and set me on my feet.

2. The appearance of his body was like sapphire, and the look of his appearance was like peridot, and the hair of his head was like snow.

3. A kidaris (a Scythian hat with long flaps usually worn by kings) was on his head and its look was like that of a rainbow.

4. His garments were purple and a golden staff was in his right hand.

5. And he said to me, "Abraham," And I said, "Here is your servant!"

6. He said, "Do not let my appearance frighten you. Nor should you let my speech trouble your soul.

7. Come with me, and I will be with you visibly until the sacrifice, but after the sacrifice I will be invisible forever more.

8. Be of good cheer, and come!"

Chapter 12

1. The two of us went together for forty days and nights, and I ate no bread and drank no water because my food and my drink was to see the angel who was with me, and to hear his voice.

2. We came to the Mount of God, Mount Horeb, and I said to the angel, "Singer to the Eternal One! I have no sacrifice and I do not know of a place with an altar on the mountain.

3. How can I bring a sacrifice?"

4. And he said to me, "Look around you." And when I looked around, there following us were all the required animals, the young heifer, the female goat, the ram, the turtle dove and the pigeon.

5. And the angel said to me, "Abraham!" And I said, "Here am I."

6. And he said, "Slaughter all these animals, and divide them into halves, place the one half against (across from/facing) the other, but do not divide (sever) the birds.

7. Give these to the men whom I will show you (that are) standing by you because these are the altar upon the Mountain, to offer a sacrifice to the Eternal (One).

8. But, the turtledove and the pigeon you will give to me because I will ascend on the wings of the birds to show you what is in the heavens, on the earth, in the sea, in the abyss, in the lower depths, in the garden of Eden, in

its rivers, and in the fullness of the universe. And you will see its circles in all."

Chapter 13

1. I did everything commanded me by the angel, and I gave the angels who had come to us the divided animals, but the angel Jaoel took the birds.

2. Then I waited until the evening sacrifice. Then and there an unclean bird flew down upon the carcasses, and I drove it away.

3. The unclean bird spoke to me and said, "Abraham, what are you doing upon these holy heights where no man eats or drinks and there is no food for man here but these heavenly beings consume everything with fire and will burn you up?

4. Forsake the man who is with you and run away because if you ascend into the heights they will destroy (kill/make an end of) you."

5. Then, when I saw the bird speaking I said to the angel: "What is this, my lord?"

6. And he said, "This is ungodliness; this is Azazel."

7. And he said to it (the bird), "Disgrace upon you, Azazel! For Abraham's portion is in heaven, but yours is upon the earth because you have chosen this for the dwelling place of your uncleanness and you have loved it.

8. Therefore the Eternal Mighty Lord forced you to dwell upon the earth, and through you every evil spirit of lies, rage, and trials came forth for the generations of ungodly men.

9. God, the Eternal and Mighty One, has not permitted the bodies of the righteous to be (end up) in your hands so that the life of the righteous and the destruction of the unclean may be assured.

10. Listen! You have no permission to tempt the righteous at all.

11. Leave this man! You cannot deceive him, because he is the enemy of you and of those who follow you and those who love what you want.

12. Behold, the garment which is heaven was formerly yours has been set aside for him, and the mortality which was his has been given over to you."

Chapter 14
1. And the angel said to me, "Abraham!"
2. And I said, "Here I am." And the angel said to me, "Know that from now on and forever the Eternal One has chosen you.
3. Be bold! I command you to use this authority against him who reviles the truth.
4. Will I not be able to revile him who has scattered about the earth the secrets of heaven and who has taken counsel against the Mighty One?
5. Say to him, "May you stoke (be kindling in) the fires of the earth's furnace!
6. Go, Azazel, into the deserted parts of the earth.
7. Your inheritance is over those who are with you, with the stars and with the men born by the clouds, whose reward you are. They exist because of you (through your being).
8. Hate is your pious act.
9. Therefore you will destroy yourself and be gone from me!"
10. And I spoke the words that the angel taught me. But the angel said to me, "Do not answer him! For God has given him power over those who answer him."
11. And the angel spoke to me again saying, "However much he speaks to you, do not answer him so that he may not get to you easily (freely).
12. The Eternal One gave him the gravity and the will. Do not answer him."
13. I did what the angel commanded me. And whatever he said to me about the fall (descent), I did not answered him.

Chapter 15

1. As the sun was setting, I beheld smoke like that of a furnace, and the angels who had the divided portions of the sacrifice came down from the top of the smoking furnace.

2. And the angel lifted me with his right hand and set me upon the right wing of the pigeon, and he sat on the left wing of the turtle dove. Neither birds had been slaughtered.

3. He flew me to the borders of the flaming fire, and we rose on many winds to the heavens which were above the firmament (sky/ theater of stars/ the sphere where the stars are stationed).

4. In the air, we ascended to a height that I could see a strong (bright) light impossible to describe.

5. In the light of a fiercely burning fire (Gehenna?), I saw many people, male in appearance. All of them were constantly changing their appearance and form. They were running as they were being changed, and they were worshipping and crying out with a sound of words that I could not recognize.

Chapter 16

1. And I said to the angel, "Why have you now brought me here?

2. I can no longer see clearly, and I am growing weak. My spirit is leaving me?"

3. And he said, "Remain close to me and do not fear.

3. He, the One you cannot see, is coming toward us now with a tremendous voice of holiness.

4. He is the Eternal One who loves you. But you yourself cannot see (look at) Him.

5. But you may find your spirit growing faint on account of the choirs of those who cry out because I am with you to strengthen you (fight against the weakness for I am here to strengthen you)."

Chapter 17

1. While he was still speaking, the fire coming toward us surrounded us and there was a voice amidst the fire like a voice of many waters, like the sound of a violent sea. And I wanted to fall down and worship. And the angel knelt down with me and worshipped.
2. However, the surface of the high place where we were standing changed constantly, inclining, rolling high and low.
3. And the angel said, "Worship, Abraham, and sing the song which I now will teach you.
4. Never stop signing it. Sing it in continuously from beginning to end. "
5. And the song which he taught me to sing had words that were appropriate to the area of heaven (sphere) we were standing in.
6. Each area (sphere) in heaven has its own song of praise, and only those who live there know how to sign it, and those on earth cannot know it or sing it.
7. They could know it only if they were taught by the messengers of heaven. And the words of that song were of a type and meaning.
8. So I bowed down since there was no solid ground on which to prostrate myself and I recited the song which he had taught me.
9. And he said, "Recite it without ceasing." And I recited, and he himself recited the song along with me.

"Eternal, Mighty, Holy God (El), God of unlimited power, Self-originated, Incorruptible, Immaculate, Without beginning, having no mother or father, Spotless, Immortal, Self-Created, Illuminated with your own light, without mother or father, self-begotten, High, radiant, Wise, Lover Of Men, Favorable, Generous, Bountiful, Jealous Over Me, Patient (compassionate), Most Merciful, Eli (my God), Eternal, Mighty, Holy Sabbath, Most Glorious El, El, El, El, (God) Jaoel (Yahoel/Joel) (Ja El/Lord God). You are he whom my soul has loved, the Guardian, Eternal, Radiant, Shining, Made of light, Voice of thunder. You appear as lightning, All seeing, you receive the prayers of those who honor you and turn away from the prayers of those who besiege you with their provoking ways. You redeem (free) those who are in the midst of the unrighteous and those who are confused among the wicked one who inhabited world in the corruptible life. You renew the life of the righteous. Before the morning light shines, you make the light shine upon your creation from the light of your face in order to bring the day on the earth. And in your heavenly dwellings there is an inexhaustible light of another kind. It is the inexpressible splendor from the lights of your face. Accept my prayer, and let it be sweet to you, and also the sacrifice which you yourself made to yourself through me who searched for you. Receive me favorably and show to me, and teach me, and make known to your servant what you have promised me."

Chapter 18

1. While I was still reciting the song, the mouth of the fire on the surface rose high in the air.

2. And I heard a voice like a roaring sea. It was not stopped by even the plethora of fire. And as the fire rose up very high I saw under the fire a throne of fire, and around it were many eyes watching.

3. They were the all-seeing ones and they were singing their song.

4. Under the throne were four radiant (on fire) Living Ones singing but they looked as if they were one creature but each one had four faces.

5. This is how they appeared and how they looked to me; each one had the face of a lion, a man, an ox and an eagle, and because of their four heads upon their bodies, they had sixteen faces.

6. Each one had three pairs of wings coming out of their shoulders, their sides, and their hips. With the wings from the shoulders they covered their faces. With the wings from their hips they covered their feet. The two middle wings were spread out and they flew erect as if standing up (straight forward).

7. Then, when they had ended their singing they looked at one another and threatened one another.

8. Then, when the angel who was with me saw that they were threatening each other he left me and went running to them. He turned the face of each living creature from the face which was opposite it so that they could not see each other's faces

9. And he taught them the song of peace which the Eternal One has in himself.

10. And while I stood alone and watched, I saw a chariot with wheels of fire behind the Living Ones.

11. Each wheel had eyes around it and it was full of eyes. Above the wheels was the throne which I had seen before. It was covered with fire, and the fire encircled it.

12. An indescribable fire contained a mighty fiery host, and I heard its holy voice like the voice of a man.

Chapter 19

1. And a voice came to me out of the middle of the fire, saying, "Abraham, "Abraham!" and I answered saying "Here am I!" And he said, "Look at the wide places (areas/expanses) which are under the firmament (sky/theater of stars) on which you now stand.

2. Notice that no other place (area/expanse) has yielded the one for whom you have searched or who has loved you."

3. While he was still talking, the areas opened up. Below me were the heavens and I saw a fire which was wide-spread. There was a light, which is the storehouse (vault) of life.

4. There was the dew that God will use to awaken the dead, the spirits of the righteous, those that had gone on before, and the spirits of those souls who are yet to be born. Judgment and righteousness, peace and blessing, and an innumerable host of angels, and the Living Ones, and the Power of the Invisible Glory sat above the Living Ones.

5. All of these were in the seventh firmament, on which I stood.

6. And I looked down from the high mountain on which I stood on to the sixth firmament, and there I saw a host of angels of pure spirit (incorporeal) without bodies, whose duty was to carry out the commands of the fiery angels who were upon the seventh firmament (some translations have the eighth firmament) , as I was standing suspended over them.

7. And I looked down on the sixth firmament and there were no other powers of any form, only the angels of pure spirit.

8. I was standing on its elevation. And on this firmament there was nothing in any form and no other host, but only the spiritual angels.

9. I saw a host on the seventh firmament and He commanded that the sixth firmament should be removed from my sight, and I saw there on the fifth firmament the powers of the stars which carry out the commands laid upon them, and the elements of the earth obeyed them.

Chapter 20

1. And the Eternal, Mighty One said to me, "Abraham, Abraham!" And I said, "Here I am!"

2. And He said to me, "Look at the stars which are beneath you, and number them for me, and then tell me their number."

3. And I said, "How can I? I am just a man made of the dust of the earth." And He said to me, " I will make your progeny a nation as large as the number of the stars and as powerful the power of the stars, and I will set these people a section (piece) for me as my own inheritance.

4. They will be distinct from those of Azazel. And yet I include Azazel in my house."

5. And I said, "Eternal and Mighty One. Let your servant speak before you and do not let your fury ignite (burn/rage) against your chosen (selected/elect) one.

6. "Look!, before you led me up, Azazel insulted (railed against/reproached) me. Since he is now not before you how can you establish (constitute/count) yourself with them?"

Chapter 21

1. Then He said to me, "Look beneath your feet at the firmament and understand the creation represented and foretold in this expanse, the creatures who exist in it, and the ages prepared after it."

2. And I looked beneath my feet and beneath the sixth heaven and saw the earth and its fruits, and what moved upon it and its beings that moved, and the host of its men, and the ungodliness of some of their souls and the righteous deeds of other souls. I saw the lower regions and the torment (perdition) in the abyss.

3. And I saw the sea and its islands, its monsters (Leviathan) and its fishes, and Leviathan and his lair, his realm (caves), and the world which lay above him, and his movements and the destructions he caused the world.

4. I saw there the streams and the rivers with their waters rising, and their winding courses. And I saw there the Garden of Eden and its fruits, the

source of the river that issues from it, the trees and their blossoms, and the men (ones) who did good deeds (behaved righteously/ justly). And I saw in it (the garden) their foods and their restfulness (blessedness).

5. And I saw there a tremendous multitude of men and women and children, half of them on the right side of the door (vision), and half of them on the left side of the door (vision).

Chapter 22
1. And I said, "Eternal, Mighty One! What is this vision of creation?"
2. And he said to me, "This is my will for what is in the light and it was good before my face.
3. After this I gave them a command and by my word and they came into existence.
4. Whatever I had decreed was to exist had already been decided (outlined in this) and all things created, which you see, had stood in front of me (in my sight) before it was created.
5. And I said, "Lord, Mighty and Eternal! Who are the people in this vision on this side and on that side?"
6. And He said to me, "Those who are on the left side are all those who existed (were born) before and after your day, some destined for judgment and restoration, and others for vengeance and estrangement at the end of the age.
7. Those on the right side of the vision are the people set a section (piece) for me. These are the ones I have prepared to be born of your lineage and to be called "my people." Some of these even come from Azazel.

Chapter 23

1. Now look again in the vision and see who it is that seduced Eve and what the fruit of the Tree was, and you will know what is to be, and how it will be for your progeny among the people at the end of the days of the age.

3. And all that you cannot understand I will make known to you for you are well-pleasing in my sight, and I will tell you of those things which are kept in my heart.

4. Then I looked into the vision, and my eyes looked at the side of the Garden of Eden, and I saw there a man of imposing height and he was great (powerful) in stature, incomparable in appearance.

5. He was embracing (entwined with) a woman who looked like his size and stature. They were standing under a tree of the Garden of Eden, and the fruit of this tree was like a bunch of grapes on a vine. Standing behind the tree was one who had the appearance of a serpent (dragon) but it had the hands and feet of a man and it had wings on its shoulders.

6. There were six pairs of wings, so that there were six wings on the right shoulder and six on the left shoulder.

7. As I continued looking, I saw the man and the woman eating the fruit from the tree. And the serpent (dragon) was holding the grapes of the tree and feeding them to the two I saw embracing each other.

8. And I said, "Who are these two that embrace, and who is this between them, and what is the fruit which they are eating, Oh, Mighty, Eternal One?"

9. And He said, "This is the world of men (this is humanity). This (one) is Adam (man), and that one, who is their desire upon the earth, is Eve.

10. But he who is between them is the ungodliness of their behavior that is sending them on the way to perdition. It is Azazel."

11. And I said, "Eternal Mighty One! Why have you given the likes of him (Azazel) the power to destroy mankind (children or generations of men) and their works upon the earth?"

12. And He said to me, " I gave him power over them who want do evil and those whom I have already hated and they will even come to love him."

13. And I said. "Eternal, Mighty One! Why did you want to bring into existence an evil that men would desire in their heart since you are angered at what was chosen by those who do useless (vain/unprofitable) things in your light (counsel/presence)?"

Chapter 24

1. He said to me, "I am angered by mankind on your account, and on account of those who will be of your family to come, because as you can see in the vision, the burden of destiny is placed upon them, and I will tell you what will be, and how much will take place in the last days. Now look at everything in the vision."

2. I looked and saw the created beings that had come into existence before me.

3. And I saw Adam and Eve and the cunning adversary who was with them; the crafty Cain, who had been influenced (led) by the adversary to break the law; and I saw the murdered (slaughtered) Abel and the destruction (lawlessness/perdition) brought on him that was caused through the lawless one.

4. And I saw there fornication and those who desired it, and its defilement and their jealousness; and the fire of the corruption in the lower depths of the earth.

5. And I saw theft and those who run after it, and the means and ways of their punishment (retribution) at the judgment of the Great Court (Assize).

6. And I saw naked men with their foreheads against each other, and their disgrace, and the passions which they had for each other, and their retribution (and the shame and harm they worked against one another).

7. And I saw Desire, and in her hand was the head of every kind of lawlessness, and her scorn and contempt and waste was assigned to destruction (perdition).

Chapter 25

1. Then I saw something that looked like an idol. It was the idol of jealousy.

2. It was carved in wood like father used to make. Its body was made of glittering bronze that covered the wood.

3. And in front of it I saw a man who was worshipping the idol, and in front of him there was an altar, and upon the altar a boy was killed as a sacrifice in the presence of the idol.

4. And I said to him, "What is this idol, and what is the altar, and who are those being sacrificed, and who is the one who performs the sacrifice, and what is the beautiful temple which I see, the are and beauty of your glory like that which lies beneath Your throne?"

5. And he said, "Hear, Abraham! This temple which you have seen, the altar and the works are my idea of the priesthood performing in the name of my glory, where every prayer (request/petition) of man will enter and live, they include the praise of kings and prophets and whatever sacrifice I decree to be made for me.

6. And He said, "Abraham, listen! What you see is the Temple, it is a copy of that which is in the heavens. It is glorious in its appearance and beauty. I will give it to the sons of men to ordain a priesthood for my glorious name. In it the prayers of man will be spoken, and sacrifices offered.)

7. I have ordained this for your people, especially those who will arise out of your lineage.

8. But the idol which you saw is the image of jealousy that will be set up by some of those who will come out of your own loins in later days.

9. And the man who sacrifices in murder is he who pollutes my Temple. These are witnesses to the final judgment, and their appointment (reward) has been set from the beginning of creation."

Chapter 26

1.. And I said, "Eternal Mighty One! Why did you establish it like this, and then proclaim the knowledge (testify) of it?" And He said to me, "Listen Abraham, and understand what I am about to say to you, and answer my question. Why did your father Terah not listen to you, and why did he not cease his idolatrous (demonic worship) practices, together with his entire house?"

2. And I said, "Eternal Mighty One, certainly because he did not want to obey me because I did not follow his (ways/deeds) works."

3. And He said to me, "The will of your father is in him (up to him), and your will is in you (up to you), and likewise the counsel of my own will is within me (up to me/in my control), and it is prepared for (has prepared) the coming days before you have any knowledge of them or can see the future with your own eyes. Now look again into the vision, and see how it will be with your children (progeny/generations)."

Chapter 27

1. And I looked and I saw the vision sway. From its left side a crowd of unbelievers (ungodly people) ran out and they captured the men, women, and children and they murdered (slaughtered like animals) most of them and others they kept as slaves. And I saw them (the killers) run towards them (the slaves) through four doors which were high with stairs and they

burned the Temple with fire, and they took and broke the holy things that were in the temple.

2. And I said, " Eternal One! Behold, my progeny, whom you have accepted, are robbed by these ungodly men. Some are killed, and others they enslave. The Temple they have burned with fire, and the beautiful things in it they have robbed and destroyed. If this is to be, why have you ripped my heart like this?"

3. And he said to me, "Listen, Abraham, all that you have seen will happen because of your progeny who will continually provoke me because of the idols that you saw, and because of the human sacrifice in the vision, through their drive and desire to do evil and there schemes in the Temple. You saw it and that is how it will be."

4. And I said, "Eternal, Mighty One! Allow these works of evil brought about by ungodliness pass by, and instead show me those who fulfilled the commandments, show me the works of righteousness. I know in truth you can do this."

5. And He said to me, "The days of the righteous (will arrive) are seen symbolized by the lives of righteous rulers who will arise, and whom I have created to rule at the appointed times. But you must know that out of them will arise others who care only for their own interests. These are symbolized by those (killers) I have already shown you.

Chapter 28

1. And I answered and said, "Mighty, Eternal One, you who are holy by your power, show mercy, I pray. Since you have brought me up here to your high place and you have showed your beloved the things about which I asked, please tell me now: Will what I saw be their lot for long?"

2. And He showed me a multitude of His people and said to me, "Because of them, I will be provoked by them through the four high doorways you

saw, and my retribution for their deeds will be accomplished. But in the fourth descent of one hundred years, which is the same as one hour of the age, the same is a hundred years, there will be evil (misfortune) among the (heathen) nations, but also for one hour there will be mercy and honor (in) among those nations.

Chapter 29

1.. And I said, " Eternal One! How long are the hours of the age?" And He said, "Twelve hours have I ordained for this present ungodly age to rule among the (heathen) nations and within your progeny, and until the end of the times it will be even as you saw. And now reckon (calculate) and understand and look again into the vision.

2. And he said, "I decreed to keep twelve periods of the impious age among the heathens and among your progeny, and what you have seen will be until the end of time."

3. And I looked and saw a Man going out from the left side of the (heathen) nations.

4. And there went men and women and children out from the side of (heathen) nations like many multitudes and they worshipped Him.

6. And while I still looked, there came many from the right side, and some of these insulted Him, and some of them even struck Him, but others worshipped Him.

7. As I watched, I saw Azazel come up to Him and he kissed Him on the face and then turned and stood behind Him.

8. Then I said, "Eternal, Mighty One! Who is this Man who is insulted and beaten, who is worshipped by the nations and kissed by Azazel?"

9. And He answered and said, "Hear Me Abraham! The Man you saw insulted and beaten and yet worshipped by many, He is the Relief/Liberty/Freedom granted for (by) the nations of people who will be

born from (out of) you in the last days, in the twelfth hour of the age of ungodliness.

10. But in the twelfth hour of my last (final) age of my fulfillment will I set up this Man from your tribe (generation), whom you saw issue from among my people, and all who follow will become like (imitate) this Man, and they will be called by me (and they will consider Him to be called by Me) and they will join the others, even those who desire to change within themselves.

11. Regarding those who emerge from the left side of the vision, the meaning is this; there will be many from the (heathen) nations who will set their hopes on (trust in) Him. But those whom you saw from your progeny on the right of the vision who insulted Him and struck Him, many will be offended because of Him, but some will worship Him. And He will test those of your progeny who have worshipped Him in the twelfth hour at the end in order to shorten the age of ungodliness.

12. Before the age of the righteous begins to grow, my judgment will come upon the (nations/heathen) lawless (wicked) peoples through the people of your progeny who have been separated to me.

13. And in those days I will bring upon all creatures of the earth ten plagues, through misfortune and disease and the groans of their bitter grief. And this will be brought upon the generations of men because of the provocation and the corruption of mankind, because they provoke me. And then the righteous men of your progeny will survive in the number (amount/count) which is kept secret by me, and will hasten the coming of the glory of My Name to that place prepared before for those you saw destroyed in the vision.

14. And they will live and be established by the sacrifices of righteousness in the age of the godly, and they will rejoice in me continually, and receive

those who return to me in repentance because their inner torment will be great for those who have wrongfully misused (mocked) them in this world.

15. And they will see the honor bestowed on those who are mine in the day of glory. Abraham, see what you have seen and hear what you have heard, and take knowledge of all that you have come to know.

16. Go to your inheritance for behold, I am with you to the age."

Chapter 30

1. While He was still speaking to me, I found myself on the earth again, and I said, " Eternal One! I am no longer in the glory on high.

2. Still there is one matter which my soul longs to know and understand that was not revealed to me."

3. And he said to me, "I will explain to you the things you desired in your heart to know which are the ten plagues that I prepared against the heathen nations, and which have been destined to begin at the passing of the twelfth hour of the age of the earth.

4. Hear therefore what I tell you because it will come to pass. The first is the sorrow and pain of (need) sickness;

5. The second, the massive burning and destruction of many cities;

6. The third, the destruction and pestilence (sickness) of animals (cattle);

7. The fourth, hunger of the whole world and its people;

8. The fifth, among the rulers, destruction by means of earthquake and the sword;

9. The sixth, the increase of hail and snow;

10. The seventh, wild bests will be their grave (animals will kill them);

11. The eighth, hunger and pestilence will change their course of destruction (alternate with destruction);

12. The ninth, punishment (execution) by the sword and flight in distress;

13. The tenth, thunder and voices and destructive earthquake.

Chapter 31

1. And then I will sound the trumpet in the air, and I will send my ELECT ONE (chosen one), and He will have all measure of my power (He will have one measure of all my power).

2. He will summon my people (who were despised) from all nations, and I will send fire upon those who have insulted them and who have ruled over them in this age. And those who have chosen my desire and kept my commandments will rejoice with celebrations (parties) over the downfall of the men who continued to followed after the idols.

3. And I will take those who have covered me with mockery and give them over to the scorn of the coming age.

4. I have prepared them to be food for the fires of Hades, and be in perpetual flight through the air of the depths of Hades (the underworld). And they will be the contents of a worm's belly (Azazel).

5. For they joined (a marital or sexual term) one to whom they had not been given to, and they abandoned the Lord who gave them strength.

Chapter 32

1. "Hear Me, Abraham, because you will see that in the seventh generation from you will go out into a strange land and the heathen will enslave and oppress them. And they leave the land of their slavery, after they have been mistreated for an hour of the age of ungodliness, and the heathen nation whom they will serve I will judge.

2. And the Lord said this too, "Have you heard, Abraham, what I told you, what your tribe will encounter in the last days?"

3. Abraham heard and accepted the words of God in his heart.

Apocalypse of Thomas

"The Apocalypse Of Thomas" is also called "The Revelation of Thomas." The differing names come from the fact that the word rendered "Apocalypse" means to reveal or make known. This is the same title given to the last book of the New Testament. Its title in Greek is best interpreted as "The Apocalypse of John," however the English book carries the title of "The Revelation of John," or simply, "Revelation."

Very little of the history of the Apocalypse of Thomas is known. The only reference to it in ancient writings seems to be a single citation by Jerome in his chronicles written in the eighth to ninth century A.D.

Two versions of the Apocalypse exist in Latin, the longer version seems to be a later development. The longer text makes use of metaphors and symbols similar to those used in the Book of Revelation. Both texts describe how the Earth will be destroyed and the dead will come back to life in the final days.

The composition of the Apocalypse of Thomas has two distinct streams of thought. It is akin to Daniel in its form of prophecy, which describes events contemporary with the author and continues them into the future; yet it is also akin to John when the text describes the signs of the end.

Historical references in the long text suggest a fifth-century date. The text speaks of a king who is a "lover of the law." The text refers to his two sons whose names begin with A and H. King Theodosius fits the bill and his sons have Latin names corresponding to the letters as follows: "The first is named with the first letter A (as in Arcadius,) the second with the eighth letter H, (as in Honorius.) The first will die before the second."

The reference to the Latin alphabet would suggest that it was the original language of composition. This would place the earliest possible date of writing (and most scholars agree) at about 300 – 400 A.D.

Several manuscripts and fragments of the Apocalypse of Thomas have been found. The text presented here is the best combination of many texts. Since some are shorter than others and many are fragments, it was thought that by combining all of the better known texts a complete, longer and more complete version could be presented.

The version presented here is based on a combination of the best manuscripts and translations found. They include the F. Wilhelm text of 1907, the E. Hauler work on the fifth century Vienna fragment, the Verona manuscript of the eighth century, the 1755 Dionisi work, 1911 Dom Bihlmeyer text from Munich, and the Anglo-Saxon Old English version at Vercelli.

THE APOCALYPSE OF THOMAS

Chapter 1

1. This begins the letter of (from) the Lord to Thomas.

2. "Hear about the things that must happen in the last times. The world will be shared between kings, then after that when the hour of the end draws near there will be seven days of great signs in heaven, and the powers of the heavens will be moved.

3. There will be famine, war and earthquakes in various places, snow, ice, and tremendous drought. There will be many open conflicts among the peoples, blasphemy, unrighteousness, envy, evil, laziness, pride and excess, and everyone will speak in the manner that he wishes.

4. And my priests will fight among themselves, and will sacrifice to me with minds of deceit. Because of this I will not look upon them. The priests will see the people forsaking the house of the Lord and turning to the world.

5. They will venture into restricted places in the house of God. And they will claim many things and places for themselves that were lost and those things and places will become subject to Caesar in the way they were given before as poll-taxes in the cities, as it is with gold and silver.

6. And the chief men of the cities will be condemned and their possessions will be brought to the treasury of the kings, and it will be filled.

7. There will be disturbances throughout all the people, and there will be death. The house of the Lord will be forsaken, and their altars will be despised, so that spiders weave their webs on them.

8. The place of holiness will be dishonored and violated, the priesthood contaminated. Distress will increase and righteousness will be overcome.

9. Happiness will die and gladness will leave. In those days evil will

abound. People will cater to those of status and wealth. Hymns will stop coming from the house of the Lord. Truth will cease. Greed will abound among the priests. No upright man nor an upright priesthood will be found.

Chapter 2

1. Near the last days a king will arise. He will be a lover of the law who will not hold office for long but he will leave two sons.

2. The first is named with the first letter A (as in Arcadius,) the second with the eighth letter H, (as in Honorius.) The first will die before the second.

(Arcadius died in 408 A.D.- Honorius in 423 A.D. The somewhat uneventful life of Arcadius is of less importance than the significant developments that occurred during his reign. Born around 377 A.D. to General Theodosius, Arcadius and his younger brother, Honorius, ruled the eastern and western halves of the Roman Empire respectively from 395. Arcadius was proclaimed Augustus in January of 383 at the age of five or six. In the following year, his younger brother was born. Honorius achieved the office of consul posterior in 386. The chance for having his own two sons ruling both halves of Rome not only seemed practical and feasible, but such an arrangement would establish their father as the head of a new dynasty. With thoughts in that direction, Honorius was made Augustus in 393 and accompanied his father west in the summer of 394. Even though Arcadius was nearing maturity and the age of consent he was placed again under the guardianship of the Prefect of the East. In January of 395, Theodosius the Great died and his two sons took theoretical control of the two halves of the Roman Empire.).

3. After this, two princes will arise to oppress the nations. Under their hands a very great famine will occur. The famine will take place in the right-hand section of the east and that nation will rise up against another nation and be driven out from their own borders.

4. Again another king will arise. He will be a deceitful man. He will order a golden image of Caesar to be made, set up, and worshipped in the house of God. Martyrdoms will be widespread.

5. Then the faith will return to the servants of the Lord, and holiness will greatly increase but so will distress and pain increase.

6. The mountains will be comforted (will comfort them?) and will drop down the sweetness of fire from its face, so that the (predestined) number of the saints may be completed.

7. After a little space of time a king will arise out of the east. He will be a lover of the law. He will cause all good and necessary things to be in supply within the house of the Lord. He will show mercy to the widows and the needy.

8. He will order that a royal gift to be given to the priests. In his days (the days of the king) there will be abundance of all things.

9. After that a king will arise, this time in the southern section of the world, and will rule for only a short time. In his days the economy will bankrupt (treasury will fail) because of the wages of the Roman soldiers. And he will order the substance of all the older citizens be taken and given to the king so it could be distributed.

Chapter 3

1. After that there will be plenty of corn and wine and oil, but a tremendous lack of money, so that it would take the substances of gold and silver to buy corn, and there will be tremendous hunger (dearth). (Hyper-inflation is indicated here.)

2. At that time the sea level will rise greatly and communications will be cut off from man to man. The kings, princes and the captains of the earth will be nervous (troubled/ fearful), and no man will speak freely.

3. Grey hairs will be seen upon boys, and the young men will not respect or

listen to the aged.

4. After that will arise another king, a deceitful man, who will rule for a short time. In his days there will be all manner of evils. There will be genocide of the race of men living in the east to Babylon (the death of the race of men from the east to Babylon).

5. Famine and death by the sword will follow from Chanaan (Canaan) to Rome. Then all the springs of water and all the wells will dry up (boil over) and be turned into dust and blood.

Chapter 4

1. The heaven will be moved and the stars will fall upon the earth. The sun will be cut in half like the moon, and the moon will not give light.

2. There will be great signs and wonders in those days when Antichrist draws near. These are the signs for those that live on the earth. In those days the pains of great and hard work like those of a woman in labor will come upon them.

3. Woe to them that build because they will not live in there buildings.

4. Woe to them that plow the ground because they labor for no cause (no results). Woe to them that marry because they will bring forth sons in the famine.

5. Woe to them that join house to house or field to field because all things will be consumed with fire. Woe to them that are not introspective (examine themselves and their actions) while time allows because after this they will be condemned forever.

6. Woe to them that turn away from the poor when he asks.

7. You will know that I am the Father most high and I am the Father of all spirits. As you will see, this is the beginning of the latter age.

Chapter 5

1. These are the seven signs of the ending of this world. There will be in all the earth famine and tremendous disease and sicknesses of vast proportions.

2. All nations will take captives and men will fall by the edge of the sword.

3. The beginning of the days of judgment will make you wonder greatly.

4. At the third hour (The Jewish day starts around 6:00 P.M.) of the first day will be a loud and powerful voice in the firmament (sky/theater of stars) of heaven, and a large cloud of blood will come down out of the north, and loud thunder and powerful lightning will follow the cloud.

5. Blood will rain down on all the earth. These are the signs of the first day. *(There is some dispute as to whether this is a literal Sunday or Monday. It is assumed by the editor that Sunday is the first day.)*

6. And on the second day there will be a loud voice in the firmament of heaven, and the earth will be moved out of its place and the portals of the eastern part of heaven will be and a great power will be sent forth as if it were belched by the portals of heaven themselves and the power will cover all the heaven even until evening and there will be fear and trembling in the world.

7. These are the signs of the second day. In the third day at about the second hour, there will be a voice in heaven, and the vast depths of the earth will sound their voices from the four corners of the earth.

8. The first heaven will be rolled up like a scroll and will vanish quickly in an instant.

9. Smoke and stench of the brimstone in the chasms will darken the day until the tenth hour. Then all men will say, "I think the end draws near, that we will die." These are the signs of the third day.

10. And on the fourth day at the first hour, the eastern section of the earth

will sound, the abyss will roar and all the earth be moved by a strong earthquake.

11. In that day all the idols of the heathen will fall along with all the buildings on earth. These are the signs of the fourth day.

12. And on the fifth day, at the sixth hour the thunder will be loud and sudden in the sky, and the stars (powers of light) and the sphere of the sun will be snatched away, and there will be total (vast) darkness over the world until evening, and the stars will be sent off their course.

13. In that day all nations will hate the world and all men will despise his life on the world. These are the signs of the fifth day.

14. On the sixth day there will be signs in heaven. At the fourth hour the firmament of heaven will be split from east to west. And the angels of the heavens will be looking out on the earth and they will open the heavens.

15. And all men will see the host of the angels above the earth looking out of heaven. Then all men will flee.

16. All men will flee to the mountains and hide themselves from the face of the righteous angels, and will say, "I wish the earth would open and swallow us!" These things will happen like this world has never seen since it was created.

17. Then they will see me coming from above in the light of my Father with the power and honor of the holy angels.

18. At my coming, the fires that border/restrain paradise will be removed because paradise is encompassed with fire.

19. And this is a perpetual fire that will consume the earth and all the elements of the world. Then they will be clothed, and be carried by the hand of the holy angels as I have told you before.

20. They will be lifted up in the air on a cloud of light, and will go with me into heaven rejoicing. They will continue in the light and honor of my Father.

21. There be gladness abounding with my Father and before the holy angels. These are the signs of the sixth day.

Chapter 6

1. Then will the spirits and souls of all men come out of paradise and will come on all the earth and every one of them will go to his own body where it is laid up, and every one of them will say, "My body lies here."
2. And when the loud voices of those spirits will be heard, like a huge earthquake (there will be a large earthquake) all over the world.
3. The mountains will be split in two from above and the rocks from beneath. Then every spirit will return into his own vessel and the bodies of the saints who have died (which have fallen asleep) will rise.
4. Then will their bodies be changed into the image and likeness and the honor of the holy angels, and into the power of the image of my holy Father.
5. Then will they be clothed with the garments of life eternal made from the cloud of light which has never been seen in this world, because that cloud came down out of the highest realm of the heaven from the power of my Father.
6. And that cloud will contain the beauty of all the spirits that have believed in me.
7. And on the seventh day at the eighth hour there will be voices in the four corners of the heaven. And all the air will be shaken, and filled with holy angels, and they will make war among the heathen all the day long. And in that day my elect will be sought out by the holy angels and saved from the destruction of the world. Then all men (unbelievers) will see that the hour of their destruction draws near.
8. These are the signs of the seventh day. And when the seven days are passed by, on the eighth day at the sixth hour there will be a sweet and tender voice in heaven from the east. Then that angel will be revealed which

has power over all the holy angels and all the angels will go out with him who is sitting upon a chariot made of the clouds of my holy Father and they will rejoice, running upon the air beneath the heaven to deliver the elect that have believed in me.

9. And they will rejoice that the destruction of this world has come.

10. Thomas, you must hear because I am the Son of God the Father and I am the father of all spirits. You must hear my signs that will come to pass at the end of this world.

11. The end of the world will come and the world will pass away before my elect depart out of the world. I will tell (have told) you openly (plainly) what will come, but when these things will come to pass even the princes of the angels do not know. It is now hidden from their sight as to what day the end will come."

12. The words of the Savior to Thomas are ended, concerning the end of this world.

4 Ezra

2 Esdras, also referred to as 4 Ezra or the Apocalypse of Ezra, was written toward the end of the first century A.D. to explain the destruction of the temple in 70 A.D. It is listed among the Apocrypha by the Catholic Church and most Protestant churches, however the Ethiopian and Russian Orthodox churches consider it to be canon.

In the years of the Renaissance and afterward heated arguments over this book inflamed emotions. Discussion regarding the book has evoked high tension and responses from the beginning. The French intelligentsia were among the most verbal. The French mystic Antoinette Bourignon said it was "the finest book in the Bible." John Floyer said it was "the best Key to all the Old and New Prophecies". Saint Jerome included the book in his Latin version of the Bible but assigned it to the apocryphal section. There were opponents also. Humphrey Prideaux considered it "a Book too absurd for the Romanists themselves to receive into their Canon."

Within the Old Testament apocrypha, 2 Esdras or 4 Ezra occupies a special place because it is dated from approximately A.D. 90, well into the New Testament era. The Vulgate version, written by Jerome, contains second and third century texts. These contain additions made by Christian writers, which made the book more acceptable to the Christian audience. 4 Ezra 7:28-9,: "For my son Jesus will be revealed with those that are with him, and they that remain will rejoice for four hundred years. After these years will my son Christ die, and all men that have life."

This makes it the only book in the Old Testament to name Jesus as the Christ. Even though many scholars believe this portion of text to be an addition made around the third to fourth century, it makes Ezra the perfect bridge between the Old testament and New testament.

Joseph B. Lumpkin

4 EZRA / 2 ESDRAS

4 Ezra Chapter 1

1: The second book of the prophet Esdras, the son of Saraias, the son of Azarias, the son of Helchias, the son of Sadamias, the son of Sadoc, the son of Achitob,

2: The son of Achias, the son of Phinees, the son of Heli, the son of Amarias, the son of Aziei, the son of Marimoth, the son of Ama, son of Uzzi, son of Borith, the son of Abishua, the son of Phinehas, the son of Eleazar,

3: The son of Aaron, of the tribe of Levi; which was captive in the land of the Medes, in the reign of Areexerxes, King of the Persians.

4: And the word of the Lord came to me, saying,

5: "Go your way, and show my people their sinful deeds, and their children their wickedness which they have done against me; that they may tell their children's children:

6: Because the sins of their fathers are increased in them for they have forgotten me, and have offered (sacrificed) to strange gods.

7: Am not I even he that brought them out of the land of Egypt, from the house of bondage? But they have provoked me to rage, and despised my counsels.

8: Pull out the hair of your head, and cast all evil upon them, for they have not been obedient to my law, but they are a rebellious people.

9: How long will I forbear them, unto whom I have done so much good?

10: Many kings have I destroyed for their sakes; Pharaoh with his servants and all his power have I beaten down.

11: All the nations have I destroyed before them, and in the east I have scattered the people of two provinces, even of Tyrus and Sidon, and have killed all their enemies.

12: Speak therefore to them, saying, Thus says the Lord,

13: I led you through the sea and in the beginning gave you a large and safe passage; I gave you Moses for a leader, and Aaron for a priest.

14: I gave you light in a pillar of fire, and great wonders have I done among you; yet you have forgotten me, says the Lord.

15: Thus, says the Almighty Lord, The quails were a gift to you; I gave you tents for your safeguard; nevertheless you murmured there,

16: And did not triumph in my name for the destruction of your enemies, but even to this day you continue to complain.

17: Where are the benefits that I have done for you? When you were hungry and thirsty in the wilderness, did you not cry to me,

18: Saying, Why have you brought us into this wilderness to kill us? It had been better for us to have served the Egyptians, than to die in this wilderness.

19: Then had I pity upon your mourning, and gave you manna to eat; so you ate angels' bread.

20: When you were thirsty, did I not cleave the rock, and waters flowed out to fill you? For the heat I covered you with the leaves of the trees.

21: I divided among you a fruitful land, I cast out the Canaanites, the Pherezites, and the Philistines, before you: what will I yet do more for you? says the Lord.

22: Thus says the Almighty Lord, When you were in the wilderness, in the river of the Amorites, being thirsty, and blaspheming my name,

23: I did not give you fire for your blasphemies, but cast a tree in the water, and made the river sweet.

24: What will I do to you, O Jacob, O Judah, who would not obey me? I will turn to other nations, and to those will I give my name, that they may keep my statutes.

25: Seeing you have forsaken me, I will forsake you also; when you desire me to be gracious to you, I will have no mercy upon you.

26: When ever you will call upon me, I will not hear you, for you have defiled your hands with blood, and your feet are swift to commit murder of men.

27: You have not forsaken me, but your own selves, says the Lord.

28: Thus says the Almighty Lord, Have I not prayed for (whished blessings on) you as a father his sons, as a mother her daughters, and a nurse her young babes,

29: That you would be my people, and I should be your God; that you would be my children, and I should be your father?

30: I gathered you together, as a hen gathers her chickens under her wings, but now, what will I do to you? I will cast you away from my face.

31: When you offer to me, I will turn my face from you for your solemn feast days, your new moons, and your circumcisions, have I forsaken.

32: I sent to you my servants the prophets, whom you have taken and slain, and torn their bodies in pieces, whose blood I will require of your hands, says the Lord.

33: Thus says the Almighty Lord, Your house is desolate, I will cast you out as the wind does the stubble (of hay).

34: And your children will not be fruitful; for they have despised my commandment, and have done the thing that is an evil before me.

35: Your houses will I give to a people that will come; which not having heard of me yet will believe me; to whom I have showed no signs, yet they will do that I have commanded them.

36: They have seen no prophets, yet they will call their sins to remembrance, and acknowledge them.

37: I take to witness the grace of the people to come, whose little ones rejoice in gladness: and though they have not seen me with bodily eyes, yet in spirit they believe the thing that I say.

38: And now, brother, behold what glory; and see the people that come from the east:

39: To whom I will give for leaders, Abraham, Isaac, and Jacob, Oseas, Amos, and Micheas, Joel, Abdias, and Jonas,

40: Nahum, and Abacuc, Sophonias, Aggeus, Zachary, and Malachy, which is called also an angel of the Lord.

4 Ezra Chapter 2

1: Thus says the Lord, I brought this people out of bondage, and I gave them my commandments by (my) menservants, the prophets; whom they would not hear, but (they) despised my counsels.

2: The mother that bare them says to them, Go your way, you children; for I am a widow and forsaken.

3: I brought you up with gladness; but with sorrow and heaviness have I lost you, for you have sinned before the Lord your God, and done that thing that is evil before him.

4: But what will I now do to you? I am a widow and forsaken; go your way, O my children, and ask mercy of the Lord.

5: As for me, O father, I call upon you for a witness over the mother of these children, which would not keep my covenant,

6: That you bring them to confusion, and their mother to a spoil, that there may be no offspring of them.

7: Let them be scattered abroad among the heathen, let their names be put out of the earth for they have despised my covenant.

8: Woe be to you, Assur, you that hide the unrighteous in you! O you wicked people, remember what I did to Sodom and Gomorrha;

9: Whose land lies in clods of pitch (clumps of tar) and heaps of ashes; even so also will I do to them that hear me not, says the Almighty Lord.

10: Thus says the Lord to Esdras, Tell my people that I will give them the Kingdom of Jerusalem, which I would have given to Israel.

11: Their glory also will I take to me, and give these the everlasting tabernacles, which I had prepared for them.

12: They will have the tree of life for an ointment of sweet savor; they will neither labor, nor be weary.

13: Go, and you will receive: pray for few days to you, that they may be shortened: the kingdom is already prepared for you: watch.

14: Take heaven and earth to witness; for I have broken the evil in pieces, and created the good; for I live, says the Lord.

15: Mother, embrace your children, and bring them up with gladness, make their feet as fast as a pillar, for I have chosen you, says the Lord.

16: And those that are dead will I raise up again from their places, and bring them out of the graves, for I have known my name in Israel.

17: Fear not, you mother of the children for I have chosen you, says the Lord.

18: For your help will I send my servants Esau and Jeremy, after whose counsel I have sanctified and prepared for you twelve trees laden with various fruits,

19: And as many fountains flowing with milk and honey, and seven mighty mountains, whereupon there grow roses and lilies, whereby I will fill your children with joy.

20: Do right to the widow, judge for (protect) the fatherless, give to the poor, defend the orphan, clothe the naked,

21: Heal the broken and the weak, do not mock the lame to scorn, defend the maimed, and let the blind man come into the clearness of my sight.

22: Keep the old and young within your walls.

23: Where ever you find the dead, take them and bury them, and I will give you the first place in my resurrection.

24: Abide still, my people, and take your rest, for your quietness still comes.

25: Nourish your children, you good nurse; establish their feet.

26: As for the servants whom I have given you, there will not one of them perish; for I will require them from among your number.

27: Do not weary: for when the day of trouble and heaviness comes, others will weep and be sorrowful, but you will be merry and have abundance.

28: The heathen will envy you, but they will be able to do nothing against you, says the Lord.

29: My hands will cover you, so that your children will not see hell.

30: Be joyful, you mother, with your children; for I will deliver you, says the Lord.

31: Remember your children that sleep (that died), for I will bring them out of the sides of the earth, and show mercy to them: for I am merciful, says the Lord Almighty.

32: Embrace your children until I come and show mercy to them: for my wells run over, and my grace will not fail.

33: I Esdras received a charge of the Lord upon the mount Oreb, that I should go to Israel; but when I came to them, they treated me as nothing and despised the commandment of the Lord.

34: Therefore I say to you, O you heathen, that hear and understand, look for your Shepherd, he will give you everlasting rest; for he is near at hand, that will come in the end of the world.

35: Be ready to receive the reward of the kingdom, for the everlasting light will shine upon you for evermore.

36: Flee the shadow of this world, receive the joyfulness of your glory: I testify of my Savior openly.

37: Receive the gift that is given to you, and be glad, giving thanks to him that has led you to the heavenly kingdom.

38: Arise up and stand, Look at the number of those that are sealed in the feast of the Lord;

39: Which have left the shadow of the world, and have received glorious garments of the Lord.

40: Take your number, O Sion, and shut up those of yours that are clothed in white, which have fulfilled the law of the Lord.

41: The number of your children, whom you longed for, is fulfilled: call on the power of the Lord, that your people, which have been called from the beginning, may be made holy.

42: I Esdras saw upon Mount Sion a great people, whom I could not number, and they all praised the Lord with songs.

43: In the midst of them there was a young man of a high stature, taller than all the rest, and upon every one of their heads he set crowns, and was more exalted; which I marveled at greatly.

44: So I asked the angel, and said, Sir, what are these?

45: He answered and said to me, These are they that have put off the mortal clothing, and put on the immortal, and have confessed the name of God: now are they crowned, and receive palms.

46: Then said I to the angel, What young person is it that crowns them, and gives them palms in their hands?

47: So he answered and said to me, It is the Son of God, whom they have confessed in the world. Then I began greatly to laud them that stood so solidly for the name of the Lord.

48: Then the angel said to me, Go your way, and tell my people what manner of things, and how great wonders of the Lord your God, you have seen.

4 Ezra Chapter 3

1: In the thirtieth year after the ruin of the city I was in Babylon, and lay troubled upon my bed, and my thoughts came up over my heart:
2: I saw the desolation of Sion, and the wealth of those dwelling at Babylon.
3: And my spirit was disturbed, so that I began to speak words full of fear to the most High, and said,
4: O Lord, who upholds rule, you spoke at the beginning, when you did plant the earth, and that yourself alone, and commanded the people,
5: And gave a body to Adam without soul, which was the workmanship of yours hands, and did breathe into him the breath of life, and he was made living before you.
6: And you lead him into paradise, which your right hand had planted, before ever the earth came forward.
7: You gave him the commandment to love your way: which he transgressed, and immediately you appointed death in him and in his generations, of whom came numberless nations, tribes, people, and kindred.
8: And every people walked after their own will, and did awful things before you, and despised your commandments.
9: And again in process of time you brought the flood upon those that dwelt in the world, and destroyed them.
10: And it came to pass in every of them, that as death was to Adam, so was the flood to these.
11: Nevertheless, you left one of them , namely, Noah with his household, from who came all righteous men.

12: And it happened, that when they that dwelt upon the earth began to multiply, and had gotten them many children, and were a great people, they began again to be more ungodly than the first.

13: Now when they lived so wickedly before you, you chose a man from among them, whose name was Abraham.

14: Him you loved, and to him only you showed your will:

15: And made an everlasting covenant with him, promising him that you would never forsake his seed.

16: And to him you gave Isaac, and to Isaac also you gave Jacob and Esau. You chose Jacob for your own, and put Esau away: and so Jacob became a great multitude.

17: And when you led his seed out of Egypt, you brought them up to Mount Sinai.

18: And bowing the heavens, you set fast the earth, moved the whole world, and made the depths to tremble, and troubled the men of that age.

19: And your glory went through four gates, of fire, and of earthquake, and of wind, and of cold; that you might give the law to the seed of Jacob, and diligence to the generation of Israel.

20: And yet you did not take away from them a wicked heart, that your law might bring forth fruit in them.

21: For the first Adam (man) bearing a wicked heart transgressed, and was overcome; and so be all that are born of him.

22: Thus infirmity was made permanent; and the law (also) in the heart of the people with the malignity of the root; so that the good departed away, and the evil still lived there.

23: So the times passed away, and the years were brought to an end: then you raised you up a servant, called David:

24: Whom you commanded to build a city to your name, and there to offer incense and offerings to you.

25: When this was done many years, then they that inhabited the city forsook you,

26: And in all things did as Adam and all his generations had done for they also had a wicked heart:

27: And so you gave your city over into the hands of yours enemies.

28: Are their deeds then any better that inhabit Babylon, that they should therefore have the dominion over Sion?

29: For when I came there, and had seen sins without number, then my soul saw many evildoers in this thirtieth year, so that my heart failed me.

30: For I have seen how you allow them sinning, and have spared wicked doers: and have destroyed your people, and have preserved yours enemies, and have not signified it.

31: I do not remember how this way may be left: Are they then of Babylon better than they of Sion?

32: Or is there any other people that knows you beside Israel? Or what generation has so believed your covenants like Jacob has?

33: And yet their reward does not appear, and their labor has no fruit: for I have gone here and there through the heathen, and I see that they flow in wealth, and think not upon your commandments.

34: Weigh our wickedness now in the balance, and theirs also that dwell the world; and so will your name no where be found but in Israel.

35: Or when was it that they which dwell upon the earth have not sinned in your sight? Or what people have so kept your commandments?

36: You will find that Israel by name has kept your precepts; but not the heathen.

4 Ezra Chapter 4

1: And the angel, whose name was Uriel, was sent to me and gave me an answer,

2: And said, Your heart has gone to far in this world, and you think to understand the way of the most High?

3: Then I said, Yea, my lord. And he answered me, and said, I am sent to show you three ways, and to set forth three comparisons before you:

4: Whereof if you can answer one, I will show you also the way that you desire to see, and I will show you from where the wicked heart came.

5: And I said, Tell on, my lord. Then said he to me, Go your way, weigh me the weight of the fire, or measure me the blast of the wind, or call me again the day that is past.

6: Then I answered and said, What man is able to do that, that you should ask such things of me?

7: And he said to me, If I should ask you how great dwellings are in the midst of the sea, or how many springs are in the beginning of the deep, or how many springs are above the firmament, or which are the outgoings of paradise:

8: I would expect you would say to me, I never went down into the deep, nor as yet into hell, neither did I ever climb up into heaven.

9: Nevertheless now have I asked you but only of the fire and wind, and of the day through which you have passed, and of things from which you can not be separated, and yet you can give me no answer.

10: He said moreover to me, Your own things, and such as are grown up with you, you do not know;

11: How should your vessel (body / mind) then be able to comprehend the way of the Highest, and the world being now outwardly corrupted to understand the corruption that is evident in my sight?

12: Then I said to him, It were better that we were not at all, than that we should live still in wickedness, and to suffer, and not to know wherefore.

13: He answered me, and said, I went into a forest into a plain, and the trees took counsel,

14: And said, Come, let us go and make war against the sea that it may depart away before us, and that we may make us more woods.

15: The floods of the sea also in like manner took counsel, and said, Come, let us go up and subdue the woods of the plain, that there also we may make us another country.

16: The thought of the wood was in vain, for the fire came and consumed it.

17: The thought of the floods of the sea came likewise to naught, for the sand stood up and stopped them.

18: If you wert judge now betwixt these two, whom would you begin to justify? Or whom would you condemn?

19: I answered and said, Verily it is a foolish thought that they both have devised, for the ground is given to the wood, and the sea also has his place to bear his floods.

20: Then he answered me, and said, You have given a right judgment, but why not judge yourself also?

21: Like the ground is given to the wood, and the sea to his floods: even so they that dwell upon the earth may understand nothing but that which is upon the earth: and he that dwells above the heavens may only understand the things that are above the height of the heavens.

22: Then I answered and said, I beseech you, O Lord, let me have understanding:

23: It was not my mind to be curious of the high things, but of such as pass by us daily, namely, wherefore Israel is given up as a criticism for the heathen, and for what cause the people whom you have loved is given over to ungodly nations, and why the law of our forefathers is brought to nothing, and the written covenants come to no effect,

24: And we pass away out of the world like grasshoppers, and our life is aw and fear, and we are not worthy to obtain mercy.

25: What will he do to his name whereby we are called? Of these things have I asked.

26: Then he answered me, and said, The more you search, the more you will marvel; for the world hastens fast to pass away,

27: And cannot comprehend the things that are promised to the righteous in time to come: for this world is full of unrighteousness and sickness.

28: But as concerning the things whereof you ask me, I will tell you. Evil is sown, but the destruction has not yet come.

29: If therefore that which is sown is not turned upside down, and if the place where the evil is sown does not pass away, then that which is sown with good cannot come.

30: For the grain of evil seed has been sown in the heart of Adam from the beginning, and how much ungodliness has it brought up to this time? And how much will it yet bring forth until the time of threshing come?

31: Ponder now by yourself, how much wicked fruit the grain of evil seed has brought forth.

32: And when the ears will be cut down, which are without number, how large of a floor will they fill?

33: Then I answered and said, How, and when will these things come to pass? Are our years few and evil?

34: And he answered me, saying, Do not try to be above the most Highest your hurry is in vain to be above him, for you have much exceeded yourself.

35: Did not the souls of the righteous also ask questions of these things in their chambers, saying, How long will I hope in this way? When comes the fruit of the floor of our reward?

36: And to these things Uriel the archangel gave them answer, and said, When the number of seeds is filled in you: for he has weighed the world in the balance.

37: By measure he has measured the times; and by number has he numbered the times; and he does not move nor stir them, until the said measure be fulfilled.

38: Then I answered and said, O Lord that upholds rule, even we all are full of sin,.

39: For our sakes peradventure it is that the floors of the righteous are not filled, because of the sins of them that dwell upon the earth.

40: So he answered me, and said, Go your way to a woman with child, and ask of her when she has fulfilled her nine months, if her womb may keep the birth any longer within her.

41: Then said I, No, Lord, she cannot. And he said to me, In the grave the chambers of souls are like the womb of a woman:

42: Like a woman that labors makes haste to escape the necessity of the travail: even so do these places haste to deliver those things that are committed to them.

43: From the beginning, look what you desire to see, it will be showed you.

44: Then I answered and said, If I have found favor in your sight, and if it is possible, and if I am worthy,

45: Show me then whether there is more to come than is past, or more past than is to come.

46: What is past I know, but what is for to come I know not.

47: And he said to me, Stand up upon the right side, and I will explain the illustration to you.

48: So I stood, and saw, and, behold, a hot burning oven passed by before me; and it when the flame was gone by I looked, and, behold, the smoke remained still.

49: After this there passed by before me a watery cloud, and sent down much rain with a storm; and when the stormy rain was past, the drops remained still.

50: Then he said to me, Think about this; as the rain is more than the drops, and as the fire is greater than the smoke; but the drops and the smoke remain behind; so the quantity which is past is greater.

51: Then I prayed, and said, I will live until that time? Or what will happen in those days?

52: He answered me, and said, As for the tokens whereof you ask me, I may tell you of them in pieces: but as touching your life, I am not sent to show you; for I do not know it.

4 Ezra Chapter 5

1: However, to share a small part with you, the days will come, that they which dwell upon earth will be taken in a great number, and the way of truth will be hidden, and the land will be barren of faith.

2: But iniquity will be increased above that which now you see, or that you have heard long ago.

3: And the land, that you see now supporting plants, will you see wasted suddenly.

4: But if the most High grants you to live, you will see after the third trumpet that the sun will suddenly shine again in the night, and the moon three time in the day:

5: And blood will drop out of wood, and the stone will have a voice, and the people will be troubled:

6: He will rule, whom they do not look for that dwell upon the earth, and the fowls will take their flight away together:

7: And the Sodomitish sea will cast out fish and make a noise at night, which many have not known: but they will all hear the voice of it.

8: There will be a confusion in many places, and the fire will be sent out again often, and the wild beasts will change their places, and women having their periods will give birth to monsters:

9: And salt waters will be found in the sweet, and all friends will destroy one another; then common sense will hide itself, and understanding withdraw itself into his secret rooms,

10: And will be sought of many, and yet not be found: then will unrighteousness and sexual passion be multiplied upon earth.

11: One land also will ask another, and say, Is righteousness that makes a man righteous gone through you? And it will say, No.

12: At the same time men will hope, but nothing will be obtain: they will labor, but their ways will not prosper.

13: I have permission to show you such things; and if you will pray again, and weep as now, and fast even days, you will hear yet greater things.

14: Then I awoke, and an extreme fearfulness went through all my body, and my mind was troubled, so that it fainted.

15: So the angel that was come to talk with me held me, comforted me, and set me up upon my feet.

16: And in the second night Salathiel the captain of the people came to me, saying, Where have you been? and why do you look so worried?

17: Do you not know that Israel is committed to you in the land of their captivity?

18: Get up then, and eat bread, and do not forsake us, as the shepherd that leaves his flock in the hands of cruel wolves.

19: Then said I to him, Go your way from me, and come not near me. And he heard what I said, and went from me.

20: And so I fasted seven days, mourning and weeping, as Uriel the angel commanded me.

21: And after seven days so it was, that the thoughts of my heart were very grievous to me again,
22: And my soul recovered the spirit of understanding, and I began to talk with the most High again,
23: And said, O Lord that upholds rule, of every wood of the earth, and of all the trees thereof, you have chosen your one and only vine:
24: And of all lands of the whole world you have chosen your one pit; and of all the flowers thereof one lily:
25: And of all the depths of the sea you have filled you one river: and of all built cities you have hallowed Sion to yourself:
26: And of all the fowls that are created you have named you one dove: and of all the cattle that are made you have provided you one sheep:
27: And among all the multitudes of people you have gotten you one people: and to this people, whom you loved, you gave a law that is approved of all.
28: And now, O Lord, why have you given this one people over to many? On this one root have you prepared others so why have you scattered your only one people among many?
29: And they who preached your promises for money, and believed not your covenants, have trodden them down.
30: If you hated your people this much, should you not punish them with your own hands?
31: Now when I had spoken these words, the angel that came to me the night before was sent to me,
32: And said to me, Hear me, and I will instruct you; hearken to the thing that I say, and I will tell you more.
33: And I said, Speak on, my Lord. Then said he to me, You are very troubled in mind for Israel's sake. Do you love that people better than he that made them?

34: And I said, No, Lord: but of very grief have I spoken: for my restraints pain me every hour, while I labor to comprehend the way of the most High, and to seek out part of his judgment.

35: And he said to me, You cannot. And I said, Why, Lord? Why was I born then? Why was my mother's womb not my grave, that I might not have seen the travail of Jacob, and the wearisome toil of the stock of Israel?

36: And he said to me, Number me the things that are not yet come, gather me together the dross that are scattered abroad, make me the flowers green again that are withered,

37: Open me the places that are closed, and bring out the winds to me that are shut up in them, show me the image of a voice: and then I will declare to you the thing that you labor to know.

38: And I said, O Lord that upholds rule, who may know these things, but he that has not his dwelling with men?

39: I am unwise: how may I then speak of these things whereof you ask me?

40: Then he said to me, Like you cannot do these things that I have spoken of, neither can you find out my judgment, or in the end the love that I have promised to my people.

41: And I said, Behold, O Lord, yet are you near to them that be reserved till the end: and what will they do that have been before me, or we that be now, or they that will come after us?

42: And he said to me, I will liken my judgment to a ring: like as there is no slackness (slowness) of the last, even so there is no swiftness of the first.

43: So I answered and said, Could you not make those that have been made, and be now, and that are to come, at once; that you might show your judgment sooner?

44: Then he answered me, and said, The creature may not rise above the maker; neither may the world hold them at once that will be created therein.

45: And I said, As you have said to your servant, that you, which gives life to all, have given life at once to the creature that you have created, and the creature bare it: even so it might now also bear them that now be present at once.

46: And he said to me, Ask the womb of a woman, and say to her, If you bring forth children, why do you it not together, but one after another? pray her therefore to bring forth ten children at once.

47: And I said, She cannot: but must do it by (its) distance (duration) of time.

48: Then said he to me, Even so have I given the womb of the earth to those that be sown in it in their times.

49: For like as a young child may not bring forth the things that belong to the aged, even so have I disposed the world which I created.

50: And I asked, and said, Seeing you have now given me the way, I will proceed to speak before you: for our mother, of whom you have told me that she is young, now draws near to age.

51: He answered me, and said, Ask a woman that bears children, and she will tell you.

52: Say to her, Why are they whom you have now brought forth like those that were before, but smaller?

53: And she will answer you, They that are born in the strength of youth are of one fashion, and they that are born in the (her) time of age, when the womb fails, are otherwise.

54: Consider therefore also, how that you are smaller than those that were before you.

55: And so are they that come after you less than you, as the creatures which now begin to be old, and have passed over the strength of youth.

56: Then I said, Lord, I beg you, if I have found favor in your sight, show your servant by whom you visit your creature.

4 Ezra Chapter 6

1: And he said to me, In the beginning, when the earth was made, before the borders of the world stood, or ever the winds blew,

2: Before it thundered and lightened, or ever the foundations of paradise were laid,

3: Before the fair flowers were seen, or ever the moveable powers were established, before the innumerable multitude of angels were gathered together,

4: Or ever the heights of the air were lifted up, before the measures of the firmament were named, or ever the chimneys in Sion were hot,

5: And in the event the present years were sought out, and or if ever the inventions of them that now sin were turned, before they were sealed that have gathered faith for a treasure:

6: I then considered these things, and they all were made through me alone, and through none other: by me also they will be ended, and by none other.

7: Then I answered and said, What will be the splitting apart of the times and when will the end of the first, and the beginning of it that follows be ?

8: And he said to me, From Abraham to Isaac, when Jacob and Esau were born of him, Jacob's hand held first the heel of Esau.

9: For Esau is the end of the world, and Jacob is the beginning of it that follows.

10: The hand of man is between the heel and the hand. Now, Esdras, do not ask any more questions.

11: I answered then and said, O Lord that upholds rule, if I have found favor in your sight,

12: I beg of you to show your servant the end of your tokens, that you showed me in part the last night.

13: So he answered and said to me, Stand up upon your feet, and hear a mighty sounding voice.

14: And it will be as it were a great motion; but the place where you stand will not be moved.

15: And therefore when it speaks be not afraid: for the word is of the end, and the foundation of the earth is understood.

16: And why? because the speech of these things trembles and is moved: for it knows that the end of these things must be changed.

17: And it happened, that when I had heard it I stood up upon my feet, and hearkened, and, behold, there was a voice that spoke, and the sound of it was like the sound of many waters.

18: And it said, Behold, the days come, that I will begin to draw near, and to visit them that dwell upon the earth,

19: And will begin to make inquisition of them, what they be that have hurt unjustly with their unrighteousness, and when the affliction of Sion will be fulfilled;

20: And when the world, that will begin to vanish away, will be finished, then will I show these tokens: the books will be opened before the firmament, and they will see all together:

21: And the children of a year old will speak with their voices, the women with child will bring forth untimely children of three or four months old, and they will live, and be raised up.

22: And suddenly will the sown places appear unsown, the full storehouses will suddenly be found empty:

23: And that trumpet will give a sound, which when every man hears, they will be suddenly afraid.

24: At that time will friends fight one against another like enemies, and the earth will stand in fear with those that dwell therein, the springs of the fountains will stand still, and in (for) three hours they will not run.

25: Whoever remains from all these that I have told you will escape, and see my salvation, and the end of your world.

26: And the men that are received will see it, who have not tasted death from their birth and the heart of the inhabitants will be changed, and turned into another meaning.

27: For evil will be put out, and deceit will be quenched.

28: As for faith, it will flourish, corruption will be overcome, and the truth, which has been so long without fruit, will be declared.

29: And when he talked with me, behold, I looked by little and little upon him before whom I stood.

30: And these words said he to me; I am come to show you the time of the night to come.

31: If you will pray even more, and fast seven days again, I will tell you greater things by day than I have heard.

32: For your voice is heard before the most High: for the Mighty has seen your righteous dealing, he has seen also your purity, which you have had ever since your youth.

33: And therefore has he sent me to show you all these things, and to say to you, "Be of good comfort and fear not

34: Do not be quick to think vain thoughts concerning the former times, or you will be hasty concerning the last times."

35: And after this I wept again, and fasted seven days in like manner, that I might fulfill the three weeks which he told me.

36: And in the eighth night was my heart vexed within me again, and I began to speak before the most High.

37: For my spirit was set on fire, and my soul was in distress.

38: And I said, O Lord, you spoke from the beginning of the creation on the first day and said; Let heaven and earth be made; and your word was a perfect work.

39: And then was the spirit, and darkness and silence were on every side; the sound of man's voice was not yet formed.

40: Then you commanded a beautiful light to come out of your treasures, that your work might appear.

41: On the second day you made the spirit of the firmament, and commanded it to section (piece) asunder, and to make a division betwixt the waters, that the one section (piece) might go up, and the other remain beneath.

42: On the third day you commanded that the waters should be gathered in the seventh part of the earth; six areas you dried up, and kept them, so that these being planted of God and tilled might serve you.

43: As soon as your word went forth the work was made.

44: For immediately there was great and innumerable fruit, and many and various pleasures for the taste, and flowers of unchangeable color, and odors of wonderful smell: and this was done the third day.

45: On the fourth day you commanded that the sun should shine, and the moon give her light, and the stars should be in order:

46: And gave them a order to do service to man that was going to be made.

47: On the fifth day you said to the seventh section, where the waters were gathered that it should bring forth living creatures, fowls and fishes: and so it came to pass.

48: For the dumb lifeless water brought forth living things at the commandment of God, that all people might praise your wondrous works.

49: Then you ordained two living creatures, one you called Behemoth, and the other (you called) Leviathan;

50: And did separate the one from the other: for the seventh section, namely, where the water was gathered together, might not hold them both.

51: To Behemoth you gave one section, which was dried up the third day, that he should dwell in the same place, where there are a thousand hills:

52: But to Leviathan you gave the seventh sections, namely, the moist; and have kept him to be devoured of whom you will, and when.

53: On the sixth day you gave commandment to the earth, that before you it should bring forth beasts, cattle, and creeping things.

54: And after these, Adam also, whom you made lord of all your creatures: of (from) him we all come, and also the people whom you have chosen.

55: All this have I spoken before you, O Lord, because you made the world for our sakes.

56: As for the other people, which also come of Adam, you have said that they are nothing, but are like to spittle: and have likened the abundance of them to a drip that falls from a vessel.

57: And now, O Lord, behold, these heathen, which have been reputed as nothing, have begun to be lords over us, and to devour us.

58: But we your people, whom you have called your firstborn, your only begotten, and your fervent lover, are given into their hands.

59: If the world now is made for our sakes, why do we not possess an inheritance with the world? How long will this last?

4 Ezra Chapter 7

1: And when I had ended speaking these words, there was sent to me the angel which had been sent to me the nights before.

2: And he said to me, Get up, Esdras, and hear the words that I have come to tell you.

3: And I said, Speak on, my God. Then said he to me, The sea is set in a wide place, that it might be deep and great.

4: But the entrance way is narrow and like a river;

5: Who then could go into the sea to look on it to rule it? If he did not go through the narrow, how could he come into the broad place?

6: There is also another thing; A city is built, and set upon a broad field, and is full of all good things.

7: The entrance of it is narrow, and is set in a dangerous place to fall, like as if there were a fire on the right hand, and on the left a deep water.

8: And one only path is between them both, even between the fire and the water, so small that there could but one man go there at once.

9: If this city now were given to a man for an inheritance, if he never will pass the danger set before it, how will he receive this inheritance?

10: And I said, Lord, that is true. Then he said to me, Even so also is Israel's portion.

11: Because for their sakes I made the world: and when Adam transgressed my statutes, then I decreed what was done.

12: Then were the entrances of this world made narrow, full of sorrow and travail: they are few and evil, full of dangers, and very painful.

13: For the entrances of the greater world were wide and safe, and brought immortal fruit.

14: Unless the living labors to enter these strait and vain things, they can never receive those things that are stored up for them.

15: Why disquiet yourself, seeing you are but a corruptible man? Why are you disturbed? You are only mortal?

16: Why have you not considered in your mind this thing that is to come, rather than that which is present?

17: Then I answered and said, O Lord that upholds rule, you have ordained in your law, that the righteous should inherit these things, but that the ungodly should perish.

18: Therefore, the righteous can endure difficult circumstances while hoping for better ones; but those who have done wickedly have suffered the difficult circumstances and will not see the easier.

19: And he said to me. There is no judge above God, and none that has understanding above the Highest.

20: For there are many that perish in this life, because they despise the law of God that is set before them. (Let many perish rather than the law…)
21: For God has plainly stated his commandment so that they that came should live, and what they should observe to avoid punishment.
22: Nevertheless they were not obedient to him; but spoke against him, and imagined vain things,
23: Deceived themselves by their wicked deeds; and said of the most High, that he does not exist; and ignore his ways:
24: But they despised His law, and denied his covenants; his statutes they have not been faithful, and have not performed his works.
25: And therefore, Esdras, for the empty are empty things, and for the full are the full things.
26: The time will come, that these tokens which I have told you will come to pass, and the bride (city) will appear, and her coming forth will be seen, that now is withdrawn from the earth.
27: And whosoever is delivered from these evils will see my wonders.
28: For my son Jesus will be revealed with those that are with him, and they that remain will rejoice for four hundred years.
29: After these years will my son Christ die, so that all men may have life.
30: And the world will be turned into the primal silence seven days, like as in the judgments of before so that no man will remain.
31: And after seven days the world that still sleeps, will be raised up, and that which is corrupt will die.
32: The earth will restore those that are asleep in her, and so will the dust those that dwell in silence, and the secret places will deliver those souls that were committed to them.
33: And the most High will appear on the seat of judgment, and misery will pass away, and the long suffering will have an end:

34: But only judgment will remain, truth will stand, and faith will grow strong.

35: And the recompense will follow, and the reward will be showed, and the good deeds will be of force, and wicked deeds will bear no rule.

36: Then I said, Abraham prayed first for the Sodomites; and Moses for the fathers that sinned in the wilderness;

37: And Jesus after him for Israel in the time of Achan;

38: And Samuel and David for the destruction: and Solomon for them that should come to the sanctuary;

39: And Helias for those that received rain and for the dead, that he might live;

40: And Ezechias for the people in the time of Sennacherib; and many pray for many.

41: Now, seeing corruption is matured, and wickedness increased, and the righteous have prayed for the ungodly; will it not be so now also?

42: He answered me, and said, This present life is not the end where much glory abides; therefore have they prayed for the weak.

43: But the day of doom will be the end of this time, and the beginning of the immortality to come, where corruption is past,

44: Hedonism is at an end, infidelity is cut off, righteousness is increased, and truth is sprung up.

45: No man are able to save him that is destroyed, nor to oppress him that has gotten the victory.

46: I answered then and said, This is my first and last saying, that it had been better not to have given the earth to Adam: or else, when it was given him, to have restrained him from sinning.

47: For what profit is it for men now in this present time to live in heaviness, and after death to look for punishment?

48: O Adam, what have you done? For though it was you that sinned, you are not fallen alone, but we all that come from you.

49: For what profit is it to us, if there be promised us an immortal time, whereas we have done the works that bring death?

50: And that there is promised us an everlasting hope, whereas ourselves being most wicked are made vain?

51: And that there are laid up for us dwellings of health and safety, whereas we have lived wickedly?

52: And that the glory of the most High is kept to defend them which have led a wary life, whereas we have walked in the most wicked ways of all?

53: And that there should be showed a paradise, whose fruit endures for ever, wherein is security and medicine, since we will not enter into it?

54: (For we have walked in unpleasant places.)

55: And that the faces of them which have used abstinence will shine above the stars, whereas our faces will be blacker than darkness?

56: For while we lived and committed sin, we did not considered that we should begin to suffer for it after death.

57: He answered me, and said, This is the condition of the battle, which man that is born upon the earth will fight;

58: That, if he is overcome, he will suffer as you have said: but if he gains victory, he will receive the thing that I say.

59: For this is the life whereof Moses spoke to the people while he lived, saying, Choose you life, that you may live.

60: Nevertheless they did not believe him, nor yet the prophets after him, no nor me which have spoken to them,

61: That there should not be such heaviness in their destruction, as will be joy over them that are persuaded to salvation.

62: I answered then, and said, I know, Lord, that the most High is called merciful, in that he has mercy upon them which are not yet come into the world,

63: And upon those also that turn to his law;

64: And that he is patient, and long suffers those that have sinned, as his creatures;

65: And that he is bountiful, for he is ready to give where it needs;

66: And that he is of great mercy, for he multiplies more and more mercies to them that are present, and that are past, and also to them which are to come.

67: For if he will not multiply his mercies, the world would not continue with them that inherit therein.

68: He forgives for if he did not do so out of his goodness so that they which have committed sin might be relieved of them, the ten thousandth part of men should not remain living.

69: And being judge, if he should not forgive them that are cured with his word, and put out the multitude of contentions,

70: There should be very few left out of an innumerable multitude.

4 Ezra Chapter 8

1: And he answered me, saying, The most High has made this world for many, but the world to come for few.

2: I will illustrate this to you, Esdras; When you ask the earth, it will say to you, that it gives much mold (rotten earth) that earthen vessels are made, but little dust that gold comes of: this is the course of this present world.

3: There are many created, but few will be saved.

4: So I said, Swallow then down, O my soul, understanding, and devour wisdom.

5: For you have agreed to give ear, and are willing to prophesy: for you have only space enough to live.

6: O Lord, if you do not permit your servant, that we may pray before you, and you give us seed to our heart, and the beginnings to our understanding, that there may come fruit of it; how will each man live that is corrupt, who bears the place of a man?

7: For you are alone, and we all one workmanship of your hands, as you have said.

8: For when the body is fashioned now in the mother's womb, and you gives it members, your creature is preserved in fire and water, and nine months your workmanship endures your creature which is created in her.

9: But that which keeps and is kept will both be preserved: and when the time comes, the womb preserved delivers up the things that grew in it.

10: For you have commanded out of the parts of the body, that is to say, out of the breasts, milk to is given, which is the fruit of the breasts,

11: That the thing which is fashioned may be nourished for a time, till you dispose it to your mercy.

12: You brought it up with your righteousness, and nurtured it in your law, and reformed it with your judgment.

13: And you will give it life as your creature, and quicken it as your work.

14: If therefore you will destroy him which with so great labor was fashioned, it is an easy thing to be ordained by your commandment, that the thing which was made might be preserved.

15: Now therefore, Lord, I will speak; touching man in general, you know best; but touching your people, for whose sake I am sorry;

16: And for yours inheritance, for whose cause I mourn; and for Israel, for whom I am heavy; and for Jacob, for whose sake I am troubled;

17: Therefore will I begin to pray before you for myself and for them: for I see the fall (failure) of us that dwell in the land.

18: But I have heard the swiftness of the judge which is to come.

19: Therefore hear my voice, and understand my words, and I will speak before you.

20: This is the beginning of the words of Esdras, before he was taken up: and I said, O Lord, you that dwell in everlastingness which watches all things from above in the heaven and in the air;

21: Whose throne is inestimable; whose glory may not be comprehended; before whom the hosts of angels stand with trembling,

22: Whose service is as knowledge of wind and fire; whose word is true, and sayings constant; whose commandment is strong, and ordinance fearful;

23: Whose look dries up the depths, and indignation makes the mountains to melt away; which are the truth witnesses.

24: O hear the prayer of your servant, and give ear to the petition of your creature.

25: For while I live I will speak, and so long as I have understanding I will answer.

26: Look not upon the sins of your people; but on them which serve you in truth.

27: Pay no attention to the devising of the wicked of the heathen, but the desire of those that keep your testimonies in afflictions.

28: Think not about those that have pretended to walk before you: but remember them, which according to your will have known your fear.

29: Let it not be your will to destroy them which have lived like beasts; but to look upon them that have clearly taught your law.

30: Take no indignation at them which are deemed worse than beasts; but love them that always put their trust in your righteousness and glory.

31: For we and our fathers do languish of such diseases but because of us sinners you will be called merciful.

32: For if you have a desire to have mercy upon us, you will be called merciful, to us namely, that have no works of righteousness.

33: For the just, which have many good works laid up with you, will out of their own deeds receive reward.

34: For what is man, that you should take displeasure at him? or what is a corruptible generation, that you should be so bitter toward it?

35: For in truth there is no man among them that is born that has not acted wickedly; and among the faithful there is none which has not acted wrongly.

36: For in this, O Lord, your righteousness and your goodness will be declared, if you be merciful to them which have not the confidence of good works.

37: Then he answered me, and said, Some things have you spoken aright, and according to your words it will be.

38: For indeed I will not think on the disposition of them which have sinned before death, before judgment, before destruction:

39: But I will rejoice over the disposition of the righteous, and I will remember also their pilgrimage, and the salvation, and the reward, that they will have.

40: Like as I have spoken now, so will it come to pass.

41: For as the husbandman sows much seed upon the ground, and plants many trees, and yet the thing that is sown good in his season cometh not up, neither doth all that is planted take root; even so is it of them that are sown in the world; they will not all be saved.

42: I answered then and said, If I have found grace, let me speak.

43: Like as the husbandman's seed perishes, if it come not up, and receive not your rain in due season; or if there come too much rain, and corrupt it:

44: Even so perishes man also, which is formed with your hands, and is called yours own image, because you are like to him, for whose sake you have made all things, and likened him to the husbandman's seed.
45: Be not wroth with us but spare your people, and have mercy upon yours own inheritance: for you are merciful to your creature.
46: Then he answered me, and said, Things present are for the present, and things to cometh for such as be to come.
47: For you come far short that you should be able to love my creature more than I. But I have often times drawn near to you, and to it, but never to the unrighteous.
48: In this also you are marvelous before the most High:
49: In that you have humbled yourself, as it becomes you, and have not judged yourself worthy to be much glorified among the righteous.
50: For many great miseries will be done to them that in the latter time will dwell in the world, because they have walked in great pride.
51: But understand you for yourself, and seek out the glory for such as be like you.
52: For to you is paradise opened, the tree of life is planted, the time to come is prepared, plenteousness is made ready, a city is built, and rest is allowed, yea, perfect goodness and wisdom.
53: The root of evil is sealed up from you, weakness and the moth is hid from you, and corruption is fled into hell to be forgotten:
54: Sorrows are passed, and in the end is showed the treasure of immortality.
55: And therefore ask no more questions concerning the multitude of them that perish.
56: For when they had taken liberty, they despised the most High, thought scorn of his law, and forsook his ways.
57: Moreover they have trodden down his righteous,

58: And said in their heart, that there is no God; even knowing they must die.

59: For as the things said before will receive you, so thirst and pain are prepared for them, for it was not his will that men should come to nothing:

60: But they which be created have defiled the name of him that made them, and were unthankful to him which prepared life for them.

61: And therefore is my judgment now at hand.

62: These things have I not showed to all men, but to you, and a few like you. Then I answered and said,

63: Look Lord, now you showed me the multitude of wonders, which you will begin to do in the last times; but at what time, you have not showed me.

4 Ezra Chapter 9

1: He answered me then, and said, Measure the time diligently in itself and when you see some of the signs past, which I have told you before,

2: Then will you understand, that it is the very same time, wherein the Highest will begin to visit the world which he made.

3: Therefore when there will be seen earthquakes and uproars of the people in the world:

4: Then will you well understand, that the most High spoke of those things from the days that were before you, even from the beginning.

5: For like as all that is made in the world has a beginning and an end, and the end is manifest:

6: Even so the times also of the Highest have plain beginnings in wonder and powerful works, and endings in effects and signs.

7: And every one that will be saved, and will be able to escape by his works, and by faith, whereby you have believed,

8: Will be preserved from the said perils, and will see my salvation in my land, and within my borders for I have sanctified them for me from the beginning.

9: Then will they be in pitiful case, which now have abused my ways and they that have cast them away despitefully will dwell in torments.

10: For such as in their life have received benefits, and have not known me;

11: And they that have hated my law while they had yet liberty, and, when as yet place of repentance was open to them, understood not, but despised it;

12: The same must know it after death by pain.

13: And therefore be you not curious how the ungodly will be punished, and when, but enquire how the righteous will be saved, whose the world is, and for whom the world is created.

14: Then I answered and said,

15: I have said before, and now do speak, and will speak it also hereafter, that there be many more of them which perish, than of them which will be saved.

16: Like as a wave is greater than a drop.

17: And he answered me, saying, As the field is, so is also the seed; as the flowers be, such are the colors also; such as the workman is, such also is the work; and as the husbandman is himself, so is his husbandry also; for it was the time of the world.

18: And now when I prepared the world, which was not yet made, even for them to dwell in that now live, no man spoke against me.

19: For then every one obeyed but now the manners of them which are created in this world that is made are corrupted by a perpetual seed, and rid themselves by a law which is unsearchable.

20: So I considered the world, and, behold, there was peril because of the schemes and actions that were come into it.

21: And I saw, and heartily spared it, and have kept me a grape of the cluster, and a plant of a great people.

22: Let the multitude perish then which was born in vain; and let my grape be kept, and my plant; for with great labor have I made it perfect.

23: Nevertheless, if you will cease yet seven days more, (but you will not fast in them,

24: But go into a field of flowers, where no house is built, and eat only the flowers of the field; taste no flesh, drink no wine, but eat flowers only);

25: And pray to the Highest continually, then will I come and talk with you.

26: So I went my way into the field which is called Ardath, as he commanded me; and there I sat among the flowers, and did eat of the herbs of the field, and the meat of the same satisfied me.

27: After seven days I sat upon the grass, and my heart was vexed within me, like as before;

28: And I opened my mouth, and began to talk before the most High, and said,

29: O Lord, you that show yourself to us, you was showed to our fathers in the wilderness, in a place where no man walks, in a barren place, when they came out of Egypt.

30: And you spoke saying, Hear me, O Israel; and mark my words, you seed of Jacob.

31: For, behold, I sow my law in you, and it will bring fruit in you, and you will be honored in it for ever.

32: But our fathers, who received the law, kept it not, and observed not your ordinances; and though the fruit of your law did not perish, neither could it, for it was yours;

33: Yet they that received it perished, because they kept not the thing that was sown in them.

34: And, lo, it is a custom, when the ground has received seed, or the sea a ship, or any vessel meat or drink, that, that being perished wherein it was sown or cast into,

35: That thing also which was sown, or cast therein, or received, doth perish, and remains not with us but with us it has not happened so.

36: For we that have received the law perish by sin, and our heart also which received it

37: Notwithstanding the law perishes not, but remains in his force.

38: And when I spoke these things in my heart, I looked back with mine eyes, and upon the right side I saw a woman, and, behold, she mourned and wept with a loud voice, and was much grieved in heart, and her clothes were rent, and she had ashes upon her head.

39: Then let I my thoughts go that I was in, and turned me to her,

40: And said to her, Why do you weep? Why are you so grieved in your mind?

41: And she said to me, Sir, let me alone, that I may bewail myself and add to my sorrow, for I am sore vexed in my mind, and brought very low.

42: And I said to her, What ails you? Tell me.

43: She said to me, I, your servant, have been barren and had no child, though I had an husband thirty years,

44: And those thirty years I did nothing else day and night, and every hour, but make my, prayer to the Highest.

45: After thirty years God heard me, your handmaid, looked upon my misery, considered my trouble, and gave me a son; and I was very glad of him, so was my husband also, and all my neighbors: and we gave great honor to the Almighty.

46: And I nourished him with great travail.

47: So when he grew up, and came to the time that he should have a wife, I made a feast.

4 Ezra Chapter 10

1: And it so came to pass, that when my son was entered into his wedding chamber, he fell down, and died.

2: Then we all overthrew the lights, and all my neighbors rose up to comfort me so I took my rest to the second day at night.

3: And when they had all left off to comfort me, to the end I might be quiet; then rose I up by night and fled, and came hither into this field, as you see.

4: And I do now purpose not to return into the city but here to stay, and neither to eat nor drink, but continually to mourn and to fast until I die.

5: Then I left the meditations wherein I was, and spoke to her in anger, saying,

6: You foolish woman above all other, see you not our mourning, and what happens to us?

7: How that Sion, our mother, is full of all heaviness and much humbled, mourning very sore?

8: And now, seeing we all mourn and are sad, for we are all in heaviness, are you grieved for one son?

9: For ask the earth, and she will tell you, that it is she which ought to mourn for the fall of so many that grow upon her.

10: For out of her came all at the first, and out of her will all others come, and, behold, they walk almost all into destruction, and a multitude of them is utterly pulled up by the roots.

11: Who then should make more mourning than she, that has lost so great a multitude; and not you, which are sorry but for one?

12: But if you say to me, My lamentation is not like the earth's, because I have lost the fruit of my womb, which I brought forth with pains, and bare with sorrows;

13: But the earth not so for the multitude present in it according to the course of the earth is gone, as it came:

14: Then say I to you, Like as you have brought forth with labor; even so the earth also has given her fruit, namely man, ever since the beginning to him that made her.

15: Now therefore keep your sorrow to yourself, and bear with a good courage that which has befallen you.

16: For if you will acknowledge the determination of God to be just, you will both receive your son in time, and will be commended among women.

17: Go your way then into the city to your husband.

18: And she said to me, That will I not do, I will not go into the city, but here will I die.

19: So I proceeded to speak further to her, and said,

20: Do not so, but be counseled by me; for how many are the adversities of Sion? Be comforted in regard of the sorrow of Jerusalem.

21: For you see that our sanctuary is laid waste, our altar broken down, our temple destroyed;

22: Our psaltery is laid on the ground, our song is put to silence, our rejoicing is at an end, the light of our candlestick is put out, the ark of our covenant is spoiled, our holy things are defiled, and the name that is called upon us is almost profaned. Our children are put to shame, our priests are burnt, our Levites are gone into captivity, our virgins are defiled, and our wives ravished; our righteous men carried away, our little ones destroyed, our young men are brought in bondage, and our strong men are become weak;

23: And, which is the greatest of all, the seal of Sion has now lost her honor; for she is delivered into the hands of them that hate us.

24: And therefore shake off your great heaviness, and put away the multitude of sorrows, that the Mighty may be merciful to you again, and the Highest will give you rest and ease from your labor.

25: And while I was talking with her, behold, her face upon a sudden shined exceedingly, and her countenance glistered, so that I was afraid of her, and mused what it might be.

26: And, behold, suddenly she made a great cry very fearful: so that the earth shook at the noise of the woman.

27: And I looked, and, behold, the woman appeared to me no more, but there was a city built, and a large place showed itself from the foundations: then was I afraid, and cried with a loud voice, and said,

28: Where is Uriel the angel, who came to me at the first, for he has caused me to fall into many trances, and mine end is turned into corruption, and my prayer to rebuke?

29: And as I was speaking these words behold, he came to me, and looked upon me.

30: And, lo, I lay as one that was dead, and mine understanding was taken from me and he took me by the right hand, and comforted me, and set me upon my feet, and said to me,

31: What ails you? And why are you so disquieted? And why is your understanding troubled, and the thoughts of your heart?

32: And I said, Because you have forsaken me, and yet I did according to your words, and I went into the field, and, lo, I have seen, and yet see, that I am not able to express.

33: And he said to me, Stand up manfully, and I will advise you.

34: Then said I, Speak on, my lord, in me; only forsake me not, lest I die frustrated of my hope.

35: For I have seen that I knew not, and hear that I do not know.

36: Or is my sense deceived, or my soul in a dream?

37: Now therefore I beseech you that you will show your servant of this vision.

38: He answered me then, and said, Hear me, and I will inform you, and tell you wherefore you are afraid; for the Highest will reveal many secret things to you.

39: He has seen that your way is right; for that you sorrow continually for your people, and make great lamentation for Sion.

40: This therefore is the meaning of the vision which you lately saw:

41: You saw a woman mourning and you began to comfort her:

42: But now see you the likeness of the woman no more, but there appeared to you a city built.

43: And whereas she told you of the death of her son, this is the solution:

44: This woman, whom you saw is Sion and whereas she said to you, even she whom you see as a city built,

45: Whereas, I say, she said to you, that she has been thirty years barren, those are the thirty years wherein there was no offering made in her.

46: But after thirty years Solomon built the city and offered offerings: and then bare the barren a son.

47: And whereas she told you that she nourished him with labor: that was the dwelling in Jerusalem.

48: But whereas she said to you, That my son coming into his marriage chamber happened to have a fail, and died: this was the destruction that came to Jerusalem.

49: And, behold, you saw her likeness, and because she mourned for her son, you began to comfort her: and of these things which have chanced, these are to be opened to you.

50: For now the most High sees that you are truly grieved, and allow from your whole heart for her, so has he showed you the brightness of her glory, and the pleasantness of her beauty:

51: And therefore I asked you to remain in the field where no house was built:

52: For I knew that the Highest would show this to you.

53: Therefore I commanded you to go into the field, where no foundation of any building was.

54: For in the place wherein the Highest begins to show his city, there can no man's building be able to stand.

55: And therefore fear not, let not yours heart be affrighted, but go your way in, and see the beauty and greatness of the building, as much as yours eyes be able to see:

56: And then will you hear as much as yours ears may comprehend.

57: For you are blessed above many other, and are called with the Highest; and so are but few.

58: But tomorrow at night you will remain here;

59: And so will the Highest show you visions of the high things, which the most High will do to them that dwell upon the earth in the last days. So I slept that night and another, like as he commanded me.

4 Ezra Chapter 11

1: Then saw I a dream, and, behold, there came up from the sea an eagle, which had twelve feathered wings and three heads.

2: And I saw, and, behold, she spread her wings over all the earth, and all the winds of the air blew on her, and were gathered together.

3: And I beheld, and out of her feathers there grew other contrary feathers; and they became little feathers and small.

4: But her heads were at rest; the head in the midst was greater than the other, yet rested it with the residue.

5: Moreover I beheld, and lo, the eagle flew with her feathers, and reigned upon earth, and over them that dwelt therein.

6: And I saw that all things under heaven were subject to her, and no man spoke against her, no, not one creature upon earth.
7: And I beheld, and, lo, the eagle rose upon her talons, and spoke to her feathers, saying,
8: Watch not all at once, sleep every one in his own place, and watch by course:
9: But let the heads be preserved for the last.
10: And I beheld, and, lo, the voice went not out of her heads, but from the midst of her body.
11: And I numbered her contrary feathers, and, behold, there were eight of them.
12: And I looked, and, behold, on the right side there arose one feather, and reigned over all the earth;
13: And so it was, that when it reigned, the end of it came, and the place thereof appeared no more: so the next following stood up. and reigned, and had a great time;
14: And it happened, that when it reigned, the end of it came also, like as the first, so that it appeared no more.
15: Then came there a voice to it, and said,
16: Hear you that have borne rule over the earth so long, this I say to you, before you begin to appear no more,
17: There will none after you attain to your time, neither to the half thereof.
18: Then arose the third, and reigned as the others before, and appeared no more also.
19: So went it with all the residue one after another, as that every one reigned, and then appeared no more.
20: Then I beheld, and, lo, in process of time the feathers that followed stood up upon the right side, that they might rule also; and some of them ruled, but within a while they appeared no more:

21: For some of them were set up, but ruled not.

22: After this I looked, and, behold, the twelve feathers appeared no more, nor the two little feathers:

23: And there was no more upon the eagle's body, but three heads that rested, and six little wings.

24: Then saw I also that two little feathers divided themselves from the six, and remained under the head that was upon the right side; for the four continued in their place.

25: And I beheld, and, lo, the feathers that were under the wing thought to set up themselves and to have the rule.

26: And I beheld, and, lo, there was one set up, but shortly it appeared no more.

27: And the second was sooner away than the first.

28: And I beheld, and, lo, the two that remained thought also in themselves to reign.

29: And when they so thought, behold, there awaked one of the heads that were at rest, namely, it that was in the midst; for that was greater than the two other heads.

30: And then I saw that the two other heads were joined with it.

31: And, behold, the head was turned with them that were with it, and did eat up the two feathers under the wing that would have reigned.

32: But this head put the whole earth in fear, and bare rule in it over all those that dwelt upon the earth with much oppression; and it had the governance of the world more than all the wings that had been.

33: And after this I beheld, and, lo, the head that was in the midst suddenly appeared no more, like as the wings.

34: But there remained the two heads, which also in like sort ruled upon the earth, and over those that dwelt therein.

35: And I beheld, and, lo, the head upon the right side devoured it that was upon the left side.
36: Then I head a voice, which said to me, Look before you, and consider the thing that you see.
37: And I beheld, and lo, as it were a roaring lion chased out of the wood: and I saw that he sent out a man's voice to the eagle, and said,
38: Hear you, I will talk with you, and the Highest will say to you,
39: Are not you it that remain of the four beasts, whom I made to reign in my world, that the end of their times might come through them?
40: And the fourth came, and overcame all the beasts that were past, and had power over the world with great fearfulness, and over the whole compass of the earth with much wicked oppression; and so long time dwelt he upon the earth with deceit.
41: For the earth have you not judged with truth.
42: For you have afflicted the meek, you have hurt the peaceable, you have loved liars, and destroyed the dwellings of them that brought forth fruit, and have cast down the walls of such as did you no harm.
43: Therefore is your wrongful dealing come up to the Highest, and your pride to the Mighty.
44: The Highest also has looked upon the proud times, and, behold, they are ended, and his abominations are fulfilled.
45: And therefore appear no more, you eagle, nor your horrible wings, nor your wicked feathers nor your malicious heads, nor your hurtful claws, nor all your vain body:
46: That all the earth may be refreshed, and may return, being delivered from your violence, and that she may hope for the judgment and mercy of him that made her.

4 Ezra Chapter 12

1: And while the lion spoke these words to the eagle, I saw,

2: And, behold, the head that remained and the four wings appeared no more, and the two went to it and set themselves up to reign, and their kingdom was small, and fill of uproar.

3: And I saw, and, behold, they appeared no more, and the whole body of the eagle was burnt so that the earth was in great fear: then awaked I out of the trouble and trance of my mind, and from great fear, and said to my spirit,

4: Lo, this have you done to me, in that you search out the ways of the Highest.

5: Lo, yet am I weary in my mind, and very weak in my spirit; and little strength is there in me, for the great fear wherewith I was afflicted this night.

6: Therefore will I now beseech the Highest, that he will comfort me to the end.

7: And I said, Lord that upholds rule, if I have found grace before your sight, and if I am justified with you before many others, and if my prayer indeed be come up before your face;

8: Comfort me then, and show me your servant the interpretation and plain difference of this fearful vision, that you may perfectly comfort my soul.

9: For you have judged me worthy to show me the last times.

10: And he said to me, This is the interpretation of the vision:

11: The eagle, whom you saw come up from the sea, is the kingdom which was seen in the vision of your brother Daniel.

12: But it was not expounded to him, therefore now I declare it to you.

13: Behold, the days will come, that there will rise up a kingdom upon earth, and it will be feared above all the kingdoms that were before it.

14: In the same will twelve kings reign, one after another:

15: Whereof the second will begin to reign, and will have more time than any of the twelve.

16: And this do the twelve wings signify, which you saw.

17: As for the voice which you heard speak, and that you saw not to go out from the heads but from the midst of the body thereof, this is the interpretation:

18: That after the time of that kingdom there will arise great strivings, and it will stand in peril of failing: nevertheless it will not then fall, but will be restored again to his beginning.

19: And whereas you saw the eight small under feathers sticking to her wings, this is the interpretation:

20: That in him there will arise eight kings, whose times will be but small, and their years swift.

21: And two of them will perish, the middle time approaching: four will be kept until their end begin to approach: but two will be kept to the end.

22: And whereas you saw three heads resting, this is the interpretation:

23: In his last days will the most High raise up three kingdoms, and renew many things therein, and they will have the dominion of the earth,

24: And of those that dwell therein, with much oppression, above all those that were before them: therefore are they called the heads of the eagle.

25: For these are they that will accomplish his wickedness, and that will finish his last end.

26: And whereas you saw that the great head appeared no more, it signifies that one of them will die upon his bed, and yet with pain.

27: For the two that remain will be slain with the sword.

28: For the sword of the one will devour the other but at the last will he fall through the sword himself.

29: And whereas you saw two feathers under the wings passing over the head that is on the right side;

30: It signifies that these are they, whom the Highest has kept to their end: this is the small kingdom and full of trouble, as you saw.

31: And the lion, whom you saw rising up out of the wood, and roaring, and speaking to the eagle, and rebuking her for her unrighteousness with all the words which you have heard;

32: This is the anointed, which the Highest has kept for them and for their wickedness to the end: he will reprove them, and will upbraid them with their cruelty.

33: For he will set them before him alive in judgment, and will rebuke them, and correct them.

34: For the rest of my people will he deliver with mercy, those that have been pressed upon my borders, and he will make them joyful until the coming of the day of judgment, whereof I have spoken to you from the beginning.

35: This is the dream that you saw, and these are the interpretations.

36: You only have been meet to know this secret of the Highest.

37: Therefore write all these things that you have seen in a book, and hide them.

38: And teach them to the wise of the people, whose hearts you know may comprehend and keep these secrets.

39: But wait you here yourself yet seven days more, that it may be showed you, whatsoever it pleases the Highest to declare to you. And with that he went his way.

40: And when all the people saw that the seven days were past, and I had not come again into the city, they gathered them all together, from the least to the greatest, and came to me, and said,

41: What have we offended you? And what evil have we done against you, that you forsake us, and sit here in this place?

42: For of all the prophets you only are left us, as a cluster of the vintage, and as a candle in a dark place, and as a haven or ship preserved from the tempest.

43: Are not the evils which are come to us sufficient?

44: If you will forsake us, how much better had it been for us, if we also had been burned in the midst of Sion?

45: For we are not better than they that died there. And they wept with a loud voice. Then I answered them, and said,

46: Be of good comfort, O Israel; and be not heavy, you house of Jacob:

47: For the Highest has you in remembrance, and the Mighty has not forgotten you in temptation.

48: As for me, I have not forsaken you, neither am I left you; but am come into this place, to pray for the desolation of Sion, and that I might seek mercy for the low estate of your sanctuary.

49: And now go your way home every man, and after these days will I come to you.

50: So the people went their way into the city, like as I commanded them:

51: But I remained still in the field seven days, as the angel commanded me; and did eat only in those days of the flowers of the field, and had my meat of the herbs

4 Ezra Chapter 13

1: And it came to pass after seven days, I dreamed a dream by night.

2: And, lo, there arose a wind from the sea, that it moved all the waves thereof.

3: And I beheld, and, lo, that man waxed strong with the thousands of heaven and when he turned his countenance to look, all the things trembled that were seen under him.

4: And when the voice went out of his mouth, all they burned that heard his voice, like as the earth fails when it feels the fire.

5: And after this I beheld, and, lo, there was gathered together a multitude of men, out of number, from the four winds of the heaven, to subdue the man that came out of the sea

6: But I beheld, and, lo, he had graved himself a great mountain, and flew up upon it.

7: But I would have seen the region or place throughout the hill was graven, and I could not.

8: And after this I beheld, and, lo, all they which were gathered together to subdue him were sore afraid, and yet did fight.

9: And, lo, as he saw the violence of the multitude that came, he neither lifted up his hand, nor held sword, nor any instrument of war:

10: But only I saw that he sent out of his mouth as it had been a blast of fire, and out of his lips a flaming breath, and out of his tongue he cast out sparks and tempests.

11: And they were all mixed together; the blast of fire, the flaming breath, and the great tempest; and fell with violence upon the multitude which was prepared to fight, and burned them up every one, so that upon a sudden of an innumerable multitude nothing was to be perceived, but only dust and smell of smoke; when I saw this I was afraid.

12: Afterward saw I the same man come down from the mountain, and call to him another peaceable Multitude.

13: And there came much people to him, whereof some were glad, some were sorry, and some of them were bound, and other some brought of them that were offered. Then was I sick through great fear, and I awakened, and said,

14: You have showed your servant these wonders from the beginning, and have counted me worthy that you should receive my prayer:

15: Show me now yet the interpretation of this dream.

16: For as I conceive in mine understanding, woe to them that will be left in those days and much more woe to them that are not left behind!

17: For they that were not left were in heaviness.

18: Now understand I the things that are laid up in the latter days, which will happen to them, and to those that are left behind.

19: Therefore are they come into great perils and many necessities, like as these dreams declare.

20: Yet is it easier for him that is in danger to come into these things, than to pass away as a cloud out of the world, and not to see the things that happen in the last days. And he answered to me, and said,

21: The interpretation of the vision will I show you, and I will open to you the thing that you have required.

22: Whereas you have spoken of them that are left behind, this is the interpretation:

23: He that will endure the peril in that time has kept himself: they that be fallen into danger are such as have works, and faith toward the Almighty.

24: Know this therefore, that they which be left behind are more blessed than they that be dead.

25: This is the meaning of the vision: Whereas you saw a man coming up from the midst of the sea:

26: The same is he whom God the Highest has kept a great season, which by his own self will deliver his creature: and he will order them that are left behind.

27: And whereas you saw, that out of his mouth there came as a blast of wind, and fire, and storm;

28: And that he held neither sword, nor any instrument of war, but that the rushing in of him destroyed the whole multitude that came to subdue him; this is the interpretation:

29: Behold, the days come, when the most High will begin to deliver them that are upon the earth.

30: And he will come to the astonishment of them that dwell on the earth.

31: And one will undertake to fight against another, one city against another, one place against another, one people against another, and one realm against another.

32: And the time will be when these things will come to pass, and the signs will happen which I showed you before, and then will my Son be declared, whom you saw as a man ascending.

33: And when all the people hear his voice, every man will in their own land leave the battle they have one against another.

34: And an innumerable multitude will be gathered together, as you saw them, willing to come, and to overcome him by fighting.

35: But he will stand upon the top of the Mount Sion.

36: And Sion will come, and will be showed to all men, being prepared and built, like as you saw the hill graven without hands.

37: And this my Son will rebuke the wicked inventions of those nations, which for their wicked life are fallen into the tempest;

38: And will lay before them their evil thoughts, and the torments wherewith they will begin to be tormented, which are like to a flame: and he will destroy them without labor by the law which is like to me.

39: And whereas you saw that he gathered another peaceable multitude to him;

40: Those are the ten tribes, which were carried away prisoners out of their own land in the time of Osea the king, whom Salmanasar the king of Assyria led away captive, and he carried them over the waters, and so came they into another land.

41: But they took this counsel among themselves, that they would leave the multitude of the heathen, and go forth into a further country, where never mankind dwelt,

42: That they might there keep their statutes, which they never kept in their own land.

43: And they entered into Euphrates by the narrow places of the river.

44: For the most High then showed signs for them, and held still the flood, till they were passed over.

45: For through that country there was a great way to go, namely, of a year and a half: and the same region is called Arsareth.

46: Then dwelt they there until the latter time; and now when they will begin to come,

47: The Highest will stay the springs of the stream again, that they may go through, therefore saw you the multitude with peace.

48: But those that be left behind of your people are they that are found within my borders.

49: Now when he destroys the multitude of the nations that are gathered together, he will defend his people that remain.

50: And then will he show them great wonders.

51: Then said I, O Lord that upholds rule, show me this: Wherefore have I seen the man coming up from the midst of the sea?

52: And he said to me, Like as you can neither seek out nor know the things that are in the deep of the sea; even so can no man upon earth see my Son, or those that be with him, but in the day time.

53: This is the interpretation of the dream which you saw, and whereby you only are here lightened.

54: For you have forsaken yours own way, and applied your diligence to my law, and sought it.

55: Your life have you ordered in wisdom, and have called understanding your mother.

56: And therefore have I showed you the treasures of the Highest; after other three days I will speak other things to you, and declare to you mighty and wondrous things.

57: Then went I forth into the field, giving praise and thanks greatly to the most High because of his wonders which he did in time;

58: And because he governs the same, and such things as fall in their seasons, and there I sat three days.

4 Ezra Chapter 14

1: And it came to pass upon the third day, I sat under an oak, and, behold, there came a voice out of a bush over against me, and said, Esdras, Esdras.

2: And I said, Here am I, Lord And I stood up upon my feet.

3: Then said he to me, In the bush I did manifestly reveal myself to Moses, and talked with him, when my people served in Egypt:

4: And I sent him and led my people out of Egypt, and brought him up to the mount of where I held him by me a long season,

5: And told him many wondrous things, and showed him the secrets of the times, and the end; and commanded him, saying,

6: These words will you declare, and these will you hide.

7: And now I say to you,

8: That you lay up in your heart the signs that I have showed, and the dreams that you have seen, and the interpretations which you have heard:

9: For you will be taken away from all, and from henceforth you will remain with my Son, and with such as be like you, until the times be ended.

10: For the world has lost his youth, and the times begin to wax old.

11: For the world is divided into twelve parts (pieces or section), and the ten part (pieces or section) of it are gone already, and half of a tenth section (piece):

12: And there remains that which is after the half of the tenth section (piece).

13: Now therefore set yours house in order, and reprove your people, comfort such of them as be in trouble, and now renounce corruption,

14: Let go from you mortal thoughts, cast away the burdens of man, put off now the weak nature,

15: And set aside the thoughts that are most heavy to you, and haste you to flee from these times.

16: For yet greater evils than those which you have seen happen will be done hereafter.

17: For look how much the world will be weaker through age, so much the more will evils increase upon them that dwell therein.

18: For the time is fled far away, and leasing is hard at hand: for now hasten the vision to come, which you have seen.

19: Then I answered before you, and said,

20: Behold, Lord, I will go, as you have commanded me, and reprove the people which are present, but they that will be born afterward, who will admonish them? Thus the world is set in darkness, and they that dwell therein are without light.

21: For your law is burnt, therefore no man knows the things that are done of you, or the work that will begin.

22: But if I have found grace before you, send the Holy Ghost into me, and I will write all that has been done in the world since the beginning, which were written in your law, that men may find your path, and that they which will live in the latter days may live.

23: And he answered me, saying, Go your way, gather the people together, and say to them, that they seek you not for forty days.

24: But look you prepare you many box trees, and take with you Sarea, Dabria, Selemia, Ecanus, and Asiel, these five which are ready to write swiftly;

25: And come hither, and I will light a candle of understanding in your heart, which will not be put out, till the things be performed which you will begin to write.

26: And when you have done, some things will you publish, and some things will you show secretly to the wise. Tomorrow this hour will you begin to write.

27: Then went I forth, as he commanded, and gathered all the people together, and said,

28: Hear these words, O Israel.

29: Our fathers at the beginning were strangers in Egypt, from whence they were delivered;

30: And received the law of life, which they kept not, which you also have transgressed after them.

31: Then was the land, even the land of Sion, parsed among you by lot; but your fathers, and you yourselves, have done unrighteousness, and have not kept the ways which the Highest commanded you.

32: And for as much as he is a righteous judge, he took from you in time the thing that he had given you.

33: And now are you here, and your brethren among you.

34: Therefore if so be that you will subdue your own understanding, and reform your hearts, you will be kept alive and after death you will obtain mercy.

35: For after death will the judgment come, when we will live again: and then will the names of the righteous be manifest, and the works of the ungodly will be declared.

36: Let no man therefore come to me now, nor seek after me these forty days.

37: So I took the five men, as he commanded me, and we went into the field, and remained there.

38: And the next day, behold, a voice called me, saying, Esdras, open your mouth, and drink that I give you to drink.

39: Then opened I my mouth, and, behold, he reached me a full cup, which was full as it were with water, but the color of it was like fire.

40: And I took it, and drank: and when I had drunk of it, my heart uttered understanding, and wisdom grew in my breast, for my spirit strengthened my memory:

41: And my mouth was opened, and shut no more.

42: The Highest gave understanding to the five men, and they wrote the wonderful visions of the night that were told, which they knew not and they sat forty days, and they wrote in the day, and at night they ate bread.

43: As for me. I spoke in the day, and I held not my tongue by night.

44: In forty days they wrote two hundred and four books.

45: And when the forty days were filled, that the Highest spoke, saying, The first that you have written publish openly, that the worthy and unworthy may read it:

46: But keep the seventy last, that you may deliver them only to such as be wise among the people;

47: For in them is the spring of understanding, the fountain of wisdom, and the stream of knowledge.

48: And I did so.

4 Ezra Chapter 15

1: Behold, speak you in the ears of my people the words of prophecy, which I will put in your mouth, says the Lord:

2: And cause them to be written in paper for they are faithful and true.

3: Fear not the imaginations against you, let not the incredulity of them trouble you, that speak against you.

4: For all the unfaithful will die in their unfaithfulness.

5: Behold, says the Lord, I will bring plagues upon the world; the sword, famine, death, and destruction.

6: For wickedness has exceedingly polluted the whole earth, and their hurtful works are fulfilled.

7: Therefore says the Lord,

8: I will hold my tongue no more as touching their wickedness, which they profanely commit, neither will I suffer them in those things, in which they wickedly exercise themselves. Behold, the innocent and righteous blood cries to me, and the souls of the just complain continually.

9: And therefore, says the Lord, I will surely avenge them, and receive to me all the innocent blood from among them.

10: Behold, my people is led as a flock to the slaughter: I will not suffer them now to dwell in the land of Egypt:

11: But I will bring them with a mighty hand and a stretched out arm, and strike Egypt with plagues, as before, and will destroy all the land thereof.

12: Egypt will mourn, and the foundation of it will be smitten with the plague and punishment that God will bring upon it.

13: They that till the ground will mourn for their seeds will fail through the blasting and hail, and with a fearful constellation.

14: Woe to the world and them that dwell therein!

15: For the sword and their destruction draws near, and one people will stand up and fight against another, and swords in their hands.

16: For there will be sedition among men, and invading one another; they will not regard their kings nor princes, and the course of their actions will stand in their power.

17: A man will desire to go into a city, and will not be able.

18: For because of their pride the cities will be troubled, the houses will be destroyed, and men will be afraid.

19: A man will have no pity upon his neighbor, but will destroy their houses with the sword, and spoil their goods, because of the lack of bread, and for great tribulation.

20: Behold, says God, I will call together all the kings of the earth to reverence me, which are from the rising of the sun, from the south, from the east, and Libanus; to turn themselves one against another, and repay the things that they have done to them.

21: Like as they do yet this day to my chosen, so will I do also, and recompense in their bosom. Thus says the Lord God;

22: My right hand will not spare the sinners, and my sword will not cease over them that shed innocent blood upon the earth.

23: The fire is gone forth from his rage, and has consumed the foundations of the earth, and the sinners, like the straw that is kindled.

24: Woe to them that sin, and keep not my commandments! says the Lord.

25: I will not spare them Go your way, you children, from the power, defile not my sanctuary.

26: For the Lord knows all them that sin against him, and therefore delivers he them to death and destruction.

27: For now are the plagues come upon the whole earth and you will remain in them for God will not deliver you, because you have sinned against him.

28: Behold an horrible vision, and the appearance thereof from the east;

29: Where the nations of the dragons of Arabia will come out with many chariots, and the multitude of them will be carried as the wind upon earth, that all they which hear them may fear and tremble.

30: Also the Carmanians raging in rage will go forth as the wild boars of the wood, and with great power will they come, and join battle with them, and will waste a portion of the land of the Assyrians.

31: And then will the dragons have the upper hand, remembering their nature; and if they will turn themselves, conspiring together in great power to persecute them,

32: Then these will be troubled bled, and keep silence through their power, and will flee.

33: And from the land of the Assyrians will the enemy besiege them, and consume some of them, and in their host will be fear and dread, and strife among their kings.

34: Behold clouds from the east and from the north to the south, and they are very horrible to look upon, full of rage and storm.

35: They will strike one upon another, and they will strike down a great multitude of stars upon the earth, even their own star; and blood will be from the sword to the belly,

36: And dung of men to the camel's hock.

37: And there will be great fearfulness and trembling upon earth and they that see the rage will be afraid, and trembling will come upon them.

38: And then will there come great storms from the south, and from the north, and another section (piece) from the west.

39: And strong winds will arise from the east, and will open it; and the cloud which he raised up in rage, and the star stirred to cause fear toward the east and west wind, will be destroyed.

40: The great and mighty clouds will be puffed up full of rage, and the star, that they may make all the earth afraid, and them that dwell therein; and they will pour out over every high and eminent place an horrible star,

41: Fire, and hail, and flying swords, and many waters, that all fields may be full, and all rivers, with the abundance of great waters.

42: And they will break down the cities and walls, mountains and hills, trees of the wood, and grass of the meadows, and their corn.
43: And they will go steadfastly to Babylon, and make her afraid.
44: They will come to her, and besiege her, the star and all rage will they pour out upon her: then will the dust and smoke go up to the heaven, and all they that be about her will bewail her.
45: And they that remain under her will do service to them that have put her in fear.
46: And you, Asia, that are partaker of the hope of Babylon, and are the glory of her person:
47: Woe be to you, you wretch, because you have made yourself like to her; and have decked your daughters in whoredom, that they might please and glory in your lovers, which have always desired to commit whoredom with you.
48: You have followed her that is hated in all her works and inventions: therefore says God,
49: I will send plagues upon you; widowhood, poverty, famine, sword, and pestilence, to waste your houses with destruction and death.
50: And the glory of your Power will be dried up as a flower, the heat will arise that is sent over you.
51: You will be weakened as a poor woman with stripes, and as one covered with wounds, so that the mighty and lovers will not be able to receive you.
52: Would I with jealousy have so proceeded against you, says the Lord,
53: If you had not always slain my chosen, exalting the stroke of yours hands, and saying over their dead, when you was drunken,
54: Set forth the beauty of your countenance?
55: The reward of your whoredom will be in your bosom, therefore will you receive payment in full.

56: Like as you have done to my chosen, says the Lord, even so will God do to you, and will deliver you into mischief

57: Your children will die of hunger, and you will fall through the sword: your cities will be broken down, and all yours will perish with the sword in the field.

58: They that be in the mountains will die of hunger, and eat their own flesh, and drink their own blood, for very hunger of bread, and thirst of water.

59: You as unhappy will come through the sea, and receive plagues again.

60: And in the passage they will rush on the idle city, and will destroy some portion of your land, and consume part (piece) of your glory, and will return to Babylon that was destroyed.

61: And you will be cast down by them as stubble, and they will be to you as fire;

62: And will consume you, and your cities, your land, and your mountains; all your woods and your fruitful trees will they burn up with fire.

63: Your children will they carry away captive, and, look, what you have, they will spoil it, and mar the beauty of your face.

4 Ezra Chapter 16

1: Woe be to you, Babylon and Asia! Woe be to you, Egypt and Syria!

2: Gird up yourselves with cloths of sack and hair, bewail your children, and be sorry; for your destruction is at hand.

3: A sword is sent upon you, and who may turn it back?

4: A fire is sent among you, and who may quench it?

5: Plagues are sent to you, and what is he that may drive them away?

6: May any man drive away an hungry lion in the wood? Or may any one quench the fire in stubble when it has begun to burn?

7: May one turn again the arrow that is shot of a strong archer?

8: The mighty Lord sends the plagues and who is he that can drive them away?

9: A fire will go forth from his rage and who is he that may quench it?

10: He will cast lightning, and who will not fear? He will thunder and who will not be afraid?

11: The Lord will threaten, and who will not be utterly beaten to powder at his presence?

12: The earthquakes, and the foundations thereof; the sea rises up with waves from the deep, and the waves of it are troubled, and the fishes thereof also, before the Lord, and before the glory of his power:

13: For strong is his right hand that bends the bow, his arrows that he shoots are sharp and will not miss when they are shot into the ends of the world.

14: Behold, the plagues are sent, and will not return again, until they come upon the earth.

15: The fire is kindled, and will not be put out, till it consume the foundation of the earth.

16: Like as an arrow which is shot of a mighty archer returns not backward: even so the plagues that will be sent upon earth will not return again.

17: Woe is me! woe is me! Who will deliver me in those days?

18: The beginning of sorrows and great mourning; the beginning of famine and great death; the beginning of wars, and the powers will stand in fear; the beginning of evils! What will I do when these evils will come?

19: Behold, famine and plague, tribulation and anguish, are sent as scourges for amendment.

20: But for all these things they will not turn from their wickedness, nor be always mindful of the scourges.

21: Behold, victuals will be so good and cheap upon earth, that they will think themselves to be in good case, and even then will evils grow upon earth, sword, famine, and great confusion.

22: For many of them that dwell upon earth will perish of famine; and the other, that escape the hunger, will the sword destroy.

23: And the dead will be cast out as dung, and there will be no man to comfort them: for the earth will be wasted, and the cities will be cast down.

24: There will be no man left to till the earth, and to sow it

25: The trees will give fruit, and who will gather them?

26: The grapes will ripen, and who will tread them? For all places will be desolate of men;

27: So that one man will desire to see another, and to hear his voice.

28: For of a city there will be ten left, and two of the field, which will hide themselves in the thick groves, and in the clefts of the rocks.

29: As in an orchard of olives upon every tree there are left three or four olives;

30: Or as when a vineyard is gathered, there are left some clusters of them that diligently seek through the vineyard.

31: Even so in those days there will be three or four left by them that search their houses with the sword.

32: And the earth will be laid waste, and the fields thereof will wax old, and her ways and all her paths will grow full of thorns, because no man will travel through it.

33: The virgins will mourn, having no bridegrooms; the women will mourn, having no husbands; their daughters will mourn, having no helpers.

34: In the wars will their bridegrooms be destroyed and their husbands will perish of famine.

35: Hear now these things and understand them, you servants of the Lord.

36: Behold, the word of the Lord, receive it and believe not the gods of whom the Lord spoke.

37: Behold, the plagues draw near, and are not slack.

38: As when a woman with child in the ninth month brings forth her son, with two or three hours of her birth great pains compass her womb, which pains, when the child cometh forth, they slack not a moment.

39: Even so will not the plagues be slack to come upon the earth, and the world will mourn, and sorrows will come upon it on every side.

40: O my people, hear my word and make you ready to your battle, and in those evils be even as pilgrims upon the earth.

41: He that sells, let him be as he that runs away and he that buys, as one that will lose.

42: He that occupies merchandise, as he that has no profit by it, and he that builds, as he that will not dwell therein.

43: He that sows, as if he should not reap so also he that plants the vineyard, as he that will not gather the grapes.

44: They that marry, as they that will get no children; and they that marry not, as the widowers.

45: And therefore they that labor do so in vain;

46: For strangers will reap their fruits, and spoil their goods, overthrow their houses, and take their children captives, for in captivity and famine will they get children.

47: And they that occupy their merchandise with robbery, the more they deck their cities, their houses, their possessions, and their own persons;

48: The more will I be angry with them for their sin, says the Lord.

49: Like as a whore envies a right honest and virtuous woman;

50: So will righteousness hate iniquity, when she covers herself, and will accuse her to her face, when he cometh that will defend him that diligently searches out every sin upon earth.

51: And therefore be you not like thereto, nor to the works thereof.

52: For yet a little, and iniquity will be taken away out of the earth, and righteousness will reign among you.

53: Let not the sinner say that he has not sinned, for God will burn coals of fire upon his head, which says before the Lord God and his glory, I have not sinned.

54: Behold, the Lord knows all the works of men, their imaginations, their thoughts, and their hearts;

55: Which spoke but the word, Let the earth be made and it was made; Let the heaven be made and it was created.

56: In his word were the stars made, and he knows the number of them.

57: He searches the deep, and the treasures thereof; he has measured the sea, and what it contains.

58: He has shut the sea in the midst of the waters, and with his word has he hanged the earth upon the waters.

59: He spreads out the heavens like a vault; upon the waters has he founded it.

60: In the desert has he made springs of water, and pools upon the tops of the mountains, that the floods might pour down from the high rocks to water the earth.

61: He made man, and put his heart in the midst of the body, and gave him breath, life, and understanding.

62: Yea and the Spirit of Almighty God, which made all things, and searches out all hidden things in the secrets of the earth,

63: Surely he knows your inventions, and what you think in your hearts, even them that sin, and would hide their sin.

64: Therefore has the Lord exactly searched out all your works, and he will put you all to shame.

65: And when your sins are brought forth, you will be ashamed before men, and your own sins will be your accusers in that day.

66: What will you do? Or how will you hide your sins before God and his angels?

67: Behold, God himself is the judge, fear him. Leave off from your sins, and forget your iniquities, to meddle no more with them for ever; so will God lead you forth, and deliver you from all trouble.

68: For, behold, the burning rage of a great multitude is kindled over you, and they will take away certain of you, and feed you, being idle, with things offered to idols.

69: And they that consent to them will be had in derision and in reproach, and trodden under foot.

70: For there will be in every place, and in the next cities, a great insurrection upon those that fear the Lord.

71: They will be like mad men, sparing none, but still spoiling and destroying those that fear the Lord.

72: For they will waste and take away their goods, and cast them out of their houses.

73: Then will they be known, who are my chosen; and they will be tried as the gold in the fire.

74: Hear, O you my beloved, says the Lord, behold, the days of trouble are at hand, but I will deliver you from the same.

75: Be you not afraid neither doubt; for God is your guide,

76: And the guide of them who keep my commandments and precepts, says the Lord God. Let not your sins weigh you down, and let not your iniquities lift up themselves.

77: Woe be to them that are bound with their sins, and covered with their iniquities like as a field is covered over with bushes, and the path thereof covered with thorns, that no man may travel through!

78: It is left undressed, and is cast into the fire to be consumed therewith.

2 Baruch

2 Baruch is also known as the Syriac Apocalypse of Baruch. It is part of the Jewish pseudepigraphical. It is a text written in the late first to early second century, after the fall of Jerusalem to the Romans in 70 AD.

It is not part of the canon of either the Jewish or "Western" Christian Bibles but is part of the Syriac Bible. Syriac Christianity is a distinctive and separate family. It is propagated in part by the Syriac language and culture as part of Near Eastern Christianity. The Aramaic origins borrowed much from early Judaism and Mesopotamian culture. As Christianity grew and was defined more with the Greek and Latin cultures and tongues, Syriac Christianity was persecuted.

2 Baruch is similar to Jeremiah. The lamentations and anguish seen within the text are attributed to a reaction to the fall of Jerusalem, and particularly the Temple in Jerusalem. According to the text, the Temple's sacred objects were rescued from destruction by angels, and await the temple's rebuilding.

The catastrophe of the Temple destruction caused the Jews to question their faith and their place in God's divine plan. The plundering and desecration of the temple by gentiles was tantamount to God's rejection of the Jews and called into question the very foundations of their faith.

If a religion holds that God's hand is in all things then one must resolves the question of why an omnipotent God allowed the destruction of his own temple, or the temple belonging to His people.

2 Baruch attempts to answer this question as it promises a Messiah (Anointed One) who will end the sinful ways and dominance of the heathens and re-establish the Jews as God's chosen people. Those who are

truly called will be the righteous Jews who follow the Torah and its teachings.

The text presented below is a modern rendition based in part on R. H. Charles' work done in the early 1900's. Chapter and verse divisions have been redefined to provide more logical separations. Modern wording has replaced the more archaic phrasing in the text. The result was then compared to other authoritative works and the translation modified to provide the most accurate version possible.

2 Baruch

Chapter 1

1 And it happened in the twenty-fifth year of Jeconiah, king of Judah, that the word of the Lord came to Baruch, the son of Neriah, and said to him:

2 Have you seen all that this nation (people) are doing to Me, that the evils which these two tribes which remained have done are greater than (those of) the ten tribes which were carried away captive?

3 For the former tribes were forced by their kings to commit sin, but these two of themselves have been forcing and compelling their kings to commit sin.

4 For this reason, I bring evil upon this city, and upon its inhabitants, and it will be removed from before Me for a time, and I will scatter these people among the Gentiles that they may do good to the Gentiles. And My people will be chastened, and the time will come when they will seek the prosperity of this period (their times.)

Chapter 2

1 For I have said these things to you that you may tell Jeremiah, and all those that are like you, to leave this city.

2 For your works are to this city as a firm pillar, and your prayers as a strong wall.

Chapter 3

1 And I said: O Lord, my Lord, have I come into the world for this purpose that I might see the evils of my mother?

2 Not so, my Lord. If I have found grace in Your sight, first take my spirit that I may go to my father's and not witness the destruction of my mother.

3 For two things vehemently constrain me: for I cannot resist You, and my soul cannot behold the evils of my mother.
4 But one thing I will ask in Your presence, O Lord.
5 What will there be after these things? If You destroy Your city and deliver up Your land to those that hate us, how will the name of Israel be remembered?
6 Or how will one speak of Your praises?
7 Or to whom will Your law be explained and all things therein?
8 Or will the world return to the nature it had before, and the age revert to primeval silence?
9 And will the multitude of souls be taken away, and the nature of man not again be named? And where is all that which You said to Moses regarding us?

Chapter 4
1 And the Lord said to me: This city will be delivered up for a time, and the people will be chastened during a time, And the world will not be given over to oblivion.
2 Do you think that this is that city of which I said: On the palms of My hands have I graven you?
3 This building now built in your midst is not that which is revealed with Me, that which was prepared beforehand here from the time when I took counsel to make Paradise, and showed it to Adam before he sinned, but when he transgressed the commandment it was removed from him, as also Paradise.
4 And after these things I showed it to My servant Abraham by night among the allotted victims.
5 And again also I showed it to Moses on Mount Sinai when I showed him the likeness of the tabernacle and all its vessels.

6 And now, behold, it is preserved with Me, as also is Paradise.

7 Go, therefore, and do as I command you."

Chapter 5

1 And I answered and said: So then I am destined to grieve for Zion, For your enemies will come to this place and pollute your sanctuary, and lead your inheritance into captivity; And make themselves masters of those whom You have loved. They will depart again to the place of their idols, and will boast before them: And what will You do for Your great name?

2 And the Lord said to me: My name and My glory are to all eternity; And My judgment will maintain its right in its own time.

3 You will see with your eyes that the enemy will not overthrow Zion, nor will they burn Jerusalem, but be the ministers of the Judge for the time.

4 Now go and do what I have said to you.

5 And I went and took Jeremiah, and Adu, and Seriah, and Jabish, and Gedaliah, and all the honorable men of the people, and I led them to the valley of Cedron, and I explained to them all that had been said to me.

7 And they lifted up their voices, and they all wept.

8 And we sat there and fasted until the evening.

Chapter 6

1 And it came to pass the next day that the army of the Chaldees surrounded the city, and at the time of the evening, I, Baruch, left the people and I went out and stood by the oak.

2 And I was grieving over Zion, and lamenting over the captivity which had come upon the people.

3 Suddenly a strong spirit raised me, and carried me aloft over the wall of Jerusalem.

4 And I saw four angels standing at the four corners of the city, each of them holding a torch of fire in his hands.

5 And another angel began to descend from heaven, and said to them: Hold your lamps, and do not light them till I tell you.

6 For I am first sent to speak a word to the earth, and to place in it what the Lord the Most High has commanded me.

7 And I saw him descend into the Holy of holies, and take from there the veil, and the holy ark, and the mercy-seat, and the two tables, and the holy raiment of the priests, and the altar of incense, and the forty-eight precious stones, wherewith the priest was adorned and all the holy vessels of the tabernacle.

8 And he spoke to the earth with a loud voice: Earth, earth, earth, hear the word of the mighty God, And receive what I commit to you, And guard them until the last times so that when you are ordered you may restore them, so that strangers may not get possession of them.

9 For the time comes when Jerusalem also will be delivered for a time, until it is said, that it is again restored for ever.

10 And the earth opened its mouth and swallowed them up.

Chapter 7

1 And after these things I heard that angel saying to those angels who held the lamps. Destroy it and overthrow its wall to its foundations so that the enemy should not boast and say: We have overthrown the wall of Zion, and we have burnt the place of the mighty God.

2 And you have seized the place where I had been standing before.

Chapter 8

1 Now the angels did as he had commanded them, and when they had broken up the corners of the walls, a voice was heard from the interior of the temple, after the wall had fallen, saying:

2 Enter, you enemies. Come, you adversaries; For he who kept the house has forsaken it.

3 And I, Baruch, departed.

4 And after these things happened the army of the Chaldees entered and seized the house and all that was around it.

5 And they led the people away captive, and killed some of them, and bound Zedekiah the King, and sent him to the King of Babylon.

Chapter 9

1 And I, Baruch, came, and Jeremiah, whose heart was found pure from sins, who had not been captured in the seizure of the city.

2 And we ripped our garments, we wept, and mourned, and fasted seven days.

Chapter 10

1 After seven days the word of God came to me, and said to me:

2 Tell Jeremiah to go and support the people who are led captive in to Babylon.

3 But you remain here amid the desolation of Zion, and I will show you after these days what will occur at the end of days.

4 And I said to Jeremiah as the Lord commanded me.

5 And he indeed, departed with the people; but I, Baruch, returned and sat before the gates of the temple, and I lamented with the following lamentation over Zion and said:

6 Blessed is he who was not born, or he, who having been born, has died.

7 But as for us who live, woe to us, Because we see the afflictions of Zion, and what has befallen Jerusalem.

8 I will call the Sirens from the sea, And you Lilin, (Lilin, in Jewish myth, was the daughter of Lilith, Adam's first wife, and the demon Samael who is often identified with Satan) come from the desert. And you Shedim and dragons from the forests: Awake and prepare yourselves for mourning; and take up with me the dirges, and make lamentation with me.

9 You husbandmen, sow not again; and, O earth, wherefore gives you your harvest fruits? Keep within you the sweets of your sustenance.

10 And you, vine, why further do you give your wine; for an offering will not again be made there from in Zion. Nor will the first-fruits again be offered.

11 And do you, O heavens, withhold your dew, and open not the treasuries of rain?

12 And do you, O sun, withhold the light of your rays? And do you, O moon, extinguish the multitude of your light? For why should light rise again where the light of Zion is darkened?

13 And you, you bridegrooms, enter not in. And let not the brides adorn themselves with garlands. And you women, pray not that you may bear.

14 For the barren will above all rejoice, And those who have no sons will be glad, and those who have sons will have anguish.

15 For why should they bear in pain, only to bury in grief?

16 Why again should mankind have sons? Why should the offspring of their kind again be named; where this mother is desolate, and her sons are led into captivity?

17 From this time forward speak not of beauty, and do not discuss gracefulness.

18 Moreover, you priests, take you the keys of the sanctuary and cast them into the height of heaven; and give them to the Lord and say: Guard Your house Yourself. For we are found to be false stewards.

19 And you virgins who weave fine linen and silk with gold of Ophir (the place from where the fleets of Solomon brought gold), take with haste all (these) things and cast (them) into the fire, that it may carry them to Him who made them. And the flame send them to Him who created them, lest the enemy get possession of them.

Chapter 11

1 Moreover, I, Baruch, say this against you, Babylon: If you had prospered, and Zion had dwelt in her glory, the grief to us would have been great because you would be equal to Zion.

2 But now, the grief is infinite; and the lamentation measureless because you are prospered and Zion desolate.

3 Who will be judge regarding these things? Or to whom will we complain regarding that which has befallen us? O Lord, how have You borne (it)?

4 Our fathers went to rest without grief and the righteous sleep in the earth in tranquility.

5 For they knew not this anguish, nor yet had they heard of that which had befallen us.

6 Would that you had ears, O earth, and that you had a heart, O dust. That you might go and announce in Sheol (hell / place of the dead) and say to the dead: Blessed are you more than we who live.

Chapter 12

1 But I will say what I think and I will speak against you, O land, which are prospering.

2 The noonday does not always burn, nor do the rays of the sun constantly give light.
3 Do not expect [and hope] that you will always be prosperous and rejoicing. Do not be not greatly arrogant and boastful.
4 For certainly in its own season the divine rage will awake against you, even though now in long-suffering it is held in as it were by reins.
5 And when I had said these things, I fasted seven days.

Chapter 13
1 After these things I, Baruch, was standing upon Mount Zion, and a voice came from the height and said to me:
2 Stand up on your feet, Baruch, and hear the word of the mighty God.
3 Because you have been amazed at what has befallen Zion, you will therefore be certainly preserved to the conclusion of the times, that you may be for a testimony.
4 If ever those prosperous cities say: Why has the mighty God brought upon us this retribution?
5 You say to them: You and those like you who will have seen this evil; (This is the evil) and retribution which is coming upon you and upon your people in its (destined) time that the nations may be thoroughly beaten (smitten.)
6 And then they will be in anguish.
7 And if they say at that time: For how long? You will say to them: You who have drunk the strained wine, drink also of its dregs, the judgment of the Lofty One Who has no respect of persons.
8 On this account before he had no mercy on His own sons, but afflicted them as His enemies, because they sinned, then they were disciplined so that they might be sanctified.

9 But now, you peoples and nations, you are guilty because you have always trodden down the earth, and used the creation sinfully and wrongfully.

10 For I have always benefited you and you have always been ungrateful for the beneficence.

Chapter 14

1 And I answered and said: You have shown me the method (behavior / procedure) of the times, and that which will alter these things, and You have said to me that the retribution, which has been spoken of by You, will come upon the nations.

2 And now I know that those who have sinned are many, and they have lived in prosperity, and left the world, but few nations will be left in those times, to whom those words will be said which You have said.

3 For what advantage is there in this, or what evil, worse than what we have seen happen us can we expect to see?

4 But again I will speak in Your presence: What have they profited who had knowledge before You and have not walked in vanity as the rest of the nations, and have not said to the dead: "Give us life," but always feared You, and have not left Your ways?

5 They have been carried off, nor on their account have You had mercy on Zion.

6 And if others did evil, it was due to Zion, that on account of those who do good works should be forgiven, and should not be overwhelmed on account of the works of those who practice unrighteousness.

7 But who, O Lord, my Lord, will understand Your judgment, or who will search out the profoundness of Your way?

8 Or who will think out the weight of Your path?

9 Or who will be able to think out Your incomprehensible counsel?

10 Or who of those that are born has ever found the beginning or end of Your wisdom?

11 For we have all been made like a breath. For as the breath ascends involuntarily and again dies, so it is with the nature of men, who depart not according to their own will, and know not what will befall them in the end.

12 For the righteous justly hope for the end, and without fear leave this habitation, because they have with You a store of works preserved in treasuries.

13 On this account also these without fear leave this world, and trusting with joy they hope to receive the world which You have promised them.

14 But as for us --- woe to us, who also are now shamefully treated, and at that time look forward (only) to evil.

15 But You know accurately what You have done by means of Your servants; for we are not able to understand that which is good as You are, our Creator.

16 But again I will speak in Your presence, O LORD, my Lord.

17 In ancient times there was no world with its inhabitants, You did devise and speak with a word, and with that the works of creation stood before You.

18 And You did say that You would make man the administrator of Your works, that it might be known that he was by no means made on account of the world, but the world on account of him.

19 And now I see that as the world was made on account of us, and it abides, but we, on account of whom it was made, depart.

Chapter 15

1 And the Lord answered and said to me: You are rightly amazed regarding the departure of man, but you have not judged well regarding the evils which befall those who sin.

2 And as regards what you have said, that the righteous are carried off and the impious are prospered.

3 And as regards what you have said, "Man knows not Your judgment," on this account hear, and I will speak to you, and listen, and I will cause you to hear My words.

4 Man would not rightly have understood My judgment, unless he had accepted the law, and I had instructed him in understanding.

5 But now, because he transgressed knowingly on this ground that he worked, he will be tormented.

6 And as regards what you did say regarding the righteous, that on account of them has this world come, so also again will that which is to come, come on their account.

7 For this world is to them a strife and a labor with much trouble; and that accordingly which is to come, a crown with great glory.

Chapter 16

1 And I answered and said: O LORD, my Lord, the years of this time are few and evil, and who is able in his little time to acquire that which is measureless?

Chapter 17

1 And the Lord answered and said to me: With the Most High account is not taken of much time nor of a few years.

2 For what did it profit Adam that he lived nine hundred and thirty years, and transgressed that which he was commanded?

3 Therefore the multitude of time that he lived did not profit him, but brought death and cut off the years of those who were born from him.

4 Or wherein did Moses suffer loss in that he lived only one hundred and twenty years, and inasmuch as he was subject to Him who formed him,

brought the law to the seed of Jacob, and lighted a lamp for the nation of Israel?

Chapter 18

1 And I answered and said: He that lighted has taken from the light, and there are but few that have imitated him.
2 But those many whom he has lighted have taken from the darkness of Adam and have not rejoiced in the light of the lamp.

Chapter 19

1 And He answered and said to me: So it was at that time he appointed for them a covenant. And He said to them: Behold I have placed before you life and death, and he called heaven and earth to witness against them.
2 For he knew that his time was but short, but that heaven and earth endure always.
3 But after his death they sinned and transgressed, though they knew that they had the law reproving them, and the light in which nothing could err, also the spheres (planets and stars?) which testify, and Me.
4 Now regarding everything that is, it is I that judge, but do not you take counsel in your soul regarding these things, nor afflict yourself because of those which have been.
5 For now it is the consummation of time that should be considered, whether of business, or of prosperity, or of shame, and not the beginning thereof.
6 Because if a man be prospered in his beginnings and shamefully treated in his old age, he forgets all the prosperity that he had.
7 And again, if a man is shamefully treated in his beginnings, and at his end is prospered, he remembers not again his evil treatment.

8 And again listen; though each one were prospered all that time all the time from the day on which death was decreed against those who transgress, and in his end was destroyed, everything would have been in vain.

Chapter 20

1 Therefore, behold! The days come, and the times will hasten more than the former, and the seasons will speed on more than those that are past, and the years will pass more quickly than the present (years).
2 Therefore have I now taken away Zion, that I may the more speedily visit the world in its season.
3 Therefore hold fast in your heart everything that I command you, and seal it in the recesses of your mind.
4 And then I will show you the judgment of My might, and My ways which cannot be known.
5 Go and sanctify yourself seven days, and eat no bread, nor drink water, nor speak to anyone.
6 Afterwards come to that place and I will reveal Myself to you, and speak true things with you, and I will give you commandment regarding the method (procedure / system) of the times; for they are coming and tarry not.

Chapter 21

1 And I went thence and sat in the valley of Cedron in a cave of the earth, and I sanctified my soul there, and I ate no bread, yet I was not hungry, and I drank no water, yet I thirsted not, and I was there till the seventh day, as He had commanded me.
2 And afterwards I came to that place where He had spoken with me.
3 And it came to pass at sunset that my soul (mind) took much thought, and I began to speak in the presence of the Mighty One, and said:

4 O You that made the earth, hear me; you that have fixed the firmament by the word, and have made firm the height of the heaven by the spirit, that have called from the beginning of the world that which did not yet exist, and they obey You.

5 You that have commanded the air by Your nod, and have seen those things which are to be as those things which You are (now) doing.

6 You that rule with great thought the hosts that stand before You; also the countless holy beings which You made from the beginning from the flame and fire, which stand around Your throne where You rule with indignation.

7 To You only does this belong that You should do whatsoever You wish.

8 Who causes the drops of rain to rain by number upon the earth, and alone know the conclusion of the times before they come; have respect to my prayer.

9 For You alone are able to sustain all who are, and those who have passed away, and those who are to be, those who sin, and those who are righteous as living and being past finding out.

10 For You alone live immortal and past finding out, and know the number of mankind.

11 And if in time many have sinned, yet others not a few have been righteous.

12 You know where You preserve the end of those who have sinned, or the conclusion of those who have been righteous.

13 For if there were this life only, which belongs to all men, nothing could be more bitter than this.

14 For of what profit is strength that turns to sickness, or fullness of food that turns to famine, or beauty that turns to ugliness?

15 For the nature of man is always changeable.

16 For what we were formerly now we no longer are, and what we now are we will not afterwards continue to be.

17 For if a conclusion had not been prepared for all, then their beginning would have been in vain.

18 Everything that comes from You, You informed me, and regarding everything about which I ask You, You enlighten me?

19 How long will that which is corruptible remain, and how long will the time of mortals succeed, and until what time will those who transgress in the world be polluted with much wickedness?

20 Command in mercy and accomplish all that You said You would bring, that Your might may be made known to those who think that Your long-suffering is weakness.

21 Show to those who do not recognize it, that everything that has befallen us and our city until now has been according to the long-suffering of Your power, because on account of Your name You have called us a beloved people.

22 Bring mortality to an end. Reprimand the angel of death, and let Your glory appear, and let the might of Your beauty be known, and let Sheol be sealed so that from this time forward it may not receive the dead, and let the treasuries of souls (the chamber of Guf, in Jewish mythology) restore those which are enclosed in them.

23 For there have been many years like those that are desolate from the days of Abraham and Isaac and Jacob, and of all those who are like them, who sleep in the earth, on whose account You did say that You had created the world.

24 And now quickly show Your glory, and do not put off what has been promised by You. When I had completed this prayer I was greatly weakened.

Chapter 22

1 After these things the heavens were opened, and I saw, and power was given to me, and a voice was heard from on high, and it said to me:

2 Baruch, Baruch, why are you troubled?

3 He who travels by a road but does not complete it, or who departs by sea but does not arrive at the port, can he be comforted?

4 Or he who promises to give a present to another, but does not fulfill it, is it not robbery?

5 Or he who sows the earth, but does not reap its fruit in its season, does he not lose everything?

6 Or he who plants a plant unless it grows till the time suitable to it, does he who planted it expect to receive fruit from it?

7 Or a woman who has conceived, if she bring forth untimely, does she not certainly kill her infant?

8 Or he who builds a house, if he does not roof it and complete it, can it be called a house? Tell Me that first.

Chapter 23

1, And I answered and said: "Not so, O LORD, my Lord."

2 And He answered and said to me: Why are you troubled about that which you know not, and why are you ill at ease about things of which you are ignorant?

3 You have not forgotten the people who now are and those who have passed away, so I remember those who are appointed to come.

4 Because when Adam sinned and death was the judgment against those who should be born, then the multitude of those who should be born was numbered, and for that number a place was prepared where the living might dwell and the dead might be guarded.

5 Before the appointed number is fulfilled, the creature will not live again for My spirit is the creator of life, and Sheol will receive the dead.

6 It is given to you to hear what things are to come after these times.

7 For truly My redemption has drawn near, and is not as distant as it was.

Chapter 24

1 The days come and the books will be opened in which are written the sins of all those who have sinned, and also the treasuries in which the righteousness of all those who have been righteous in creation is gathered.

2 For it will come to pass at that time that you will see, and the many that are with you, the long-suffering of the Most High, which has been throughout all generations, who has been long-suffering towards all who are born, like those who sin and those who are righteous."

3 And I answered and said: But Lord, no one knows the number of those things which have passed nor yet of those things which are to come.

4 For I know indeed that which has befallen us, but what will happen to our enemies I know not, and when You will visit Your works.

Chapter 25

1 And He answered and said to me: You too will be preserved till that time till that sign which the Most High will work for the inhabitants of the earth in the end of days.

2 This therefore will be the sign:

3 When a stupor will seize the inhabitants of the earth, and they will fall into many tribulations, and again when they will fall into great torments.

4 And it will come to pass when they say in their thoughts because of their much tribulation: The Mighty One doth no longer remember the earth yea, it will come to pass when they abandon hope, that the time will then awake.

Chapter 26

1 And I answered and said: Will that tribulation which is to be, continue a long time, and will it necessitate many years?

Chapter 27

1 And He answered and said to me: Into twelve parts (pieces or section) is that time divided, and each one of them is reserved for that which is appointed for it.
2 In the first section (piece) there will be the beginning of commotions.
3 And in the second section (piece) slayings of the great ones.
4 And in the third section (piece) the fall of many by death.
5 And in the fourth section (piece) the sending of the sword.
6 And in the fifth section (piece) famine and the withholding of rain.
7 And in the sixth section (piece) earthquakes and terrors and wanting (need for food, water, and shelter).
8 And in the eighth section (piece) a multitude of specters and attacks of the Shedim.
9 And in the ninth section (piece) the fall of fire.
10 And in the tenth section (piece) rapine and much oppression.
11 And in the eleventh section (piece) wickedness and hedonism.
12 And in the twelfth section (piece) confusion from the mingling together of all those things aforesaid.
13 For these slices of that time are reserved, and will be mingled one with another and reinforce one another.
14 For some will leave out some of their own, and receive (in its stead) from others, and some complete their own and that of others, so that those may not understand who are upon the earth in those days that this is the consummation of the times.

Chapter 28

1 Nevertheless, whosoever understands will then be wise.

2 For the measure and reckoning of that time are two parts (pieces or section) a week of seven weeks.

3 And I answered and said: It is good for a man to come and behold, but it is better that he should not come lest he fall.

4 But I will ask this also: Will he who is incorruptible despise those things which are corruptible? What happens in the case of those things which are corruptible, so that he might look only to those things which are not corruptible?

5 But if, O Lord, those things will certainly come to pass which You have foretold to me, show this to me also if indeed I have found grace in Your sight.

6 Is it in one place or in one of the sections of the earth that those things are come to pass, or will the whole earth experience them?

Chapter 29

1 And He answered and said to me: Whatever will befall the whole earth all who live will experience.

2 For at that time I will protect only those who are found in those same days in this land.

3 And when all is accomplished that was to come to pass in those sections, that the Messiah will then begin to be revealed.

4 And Behemoth will be revealed from his place and Leviathan will ascend from the sea, those two great monsters which I created on the fifth day of creation, and will have kept until that time; and then they will be food for all that are left.

5 The earth also will yield its fruit ten thousand fold and on each vine there will be a thousand branches, and each branch will produce a thousand

clusters, and each cluster produces a thousand grapes, and each grape produces a cor (a unit of measure approximately 517 pints) of wine.

6 And those who have hungered will rejoice, moreover, they will behold marvels every day.

7 For winds will go forth from before Me to bring every morning the fragrance of aromatic fruits, and at the close of the day clouds distilling the dew of health.

8 And it will come to pass at that same time that the treasury of manna will again descend from on high, and they will eat of it in those years, because these are they who have come to the end of time.

Chapter 30

1 And it will come to pass after these things, when the time of the advent of the Messiah is fulfilled, that He will return in glory.

2 Then all who have fallen asleep in hope of Him will rise again.

3 And it will come to pass at that time that the treasuries will be opened in which is preserved the number of the souls of the righteous, and they will come forth, and a multitude of souls will be seen together in one assemblage of one thought, and the first will rejoice and the last will not be grieved. For they know that the time has come of which it is said, that it is the consummation of the times.

4 But the souls of the wicked, when they behold all these things, will then waste away the more.

5 For they will know that their torment has come and their perdition has arrived."

Chapter 31

1 And after these things I went to the people and said to them:
2 Assemble to me all your elders and I will speak words to them.

3 And they all assembled in the valley of the Cedron. And I answered and said to them: Hear, O Israel, and I will speak to you, And give ear, O seed of Jacob, and I will instruct you.

4 Forget not Zion, But hold in remembrance the anguish of Jerusalem.

5 For the days come, when everything exists will become the prey of corruption and will be as though it had not been.

Chapter 32

1 But if you prepare your hearts, so as to sow in them the fruits of the law, it will protect you in that time in which the Mighty One is to shake the whole creation.

2 Because after a little time the building of Zion will be shaken in order that it may be built again.

3 But that building will not remain, but will again after a time be pulled up by the roots, and will remain desolate until the time.

4 And afterwards it must be renewed in glory, and perfected for evermore.

5 Therefore we should not be distressed so much over the evil which has now come as over that which is still to be.

6 For there will be a greater trial than these two tribulations when the Mighty One will renew His creation.

7 And now do not draw near to me for a few days, nor seek me till I come to you.

8 And when I had spoken to them all these words, that I, Baruch, went my way, and when the people saw me leaving, they lifted up their voice and lamented and said: To what place do you depart from us, Baruch, and forsake us as a father who forsakes his orphan children, and departs from them?

Chapter 33

1 Are these the commands which your companion, Jeremiah the prophet, commanded you, and said to you:

2 Look to this people till I go and make ready the rest of the brethren in Babylon, against whom has gone forth the sentence that they should be led into captivity?

3 And now if you also forsake us, it were good for us all to die before you withdraw from us.

Chapter 34

1 And I answered and said to the people: Far be it from me to forsake you or to withdraw from you, but I will only go to the Holy of Holies to inquire of the Mighty One concerning you and concerning Zion; in the hopes I should receive more illumination and after these things I will return to you.

Chapter 35

1 And I, Baruch, went to the holy place, and sat down upon the ruins and wept, and said:

2 O that mine eyes were springs, and mine eyelids a spring of tears.

3 For how will I lament for Zion, and how will I mourn for Jerusalem?

4 Because in that place where I am now prostrate, of old the high priest offered holy sacrifices; and placed thereon an incense of fragrant odors.

5 But now our glorying has been made into dust, And the desire of our soul into sand.

Chapter 36

1 And when I had said these things I fell asleep there, and I saw a vision in the night.

2 I saw a forest of trees planted on the plain, and lofty and rugged rocky mountains surrounded it, and that forest occupied much space.

3 And over beside it arose a vine, and from under it there went forth a peaceful fountain.

4 Now that fountain came to the forest and was agitated into great waves, and those waves submerged that forest, and suddenly they pulled up by the roots the greater section (area) of that forest, and overthrew all the mountains which were around it.

5 And the height of the forest began to be made low, and the top of the mountains was made low and that fountain greatly overtook it, so that it left nothing of that great forest save one cedar only.

6 Also when it had cast it down and had destroyed and pulled up by the roots the greater part of that forest, so that nothing was left of it, nor could its place be recognized, then that vine began to come with the fountain in peace and great tranquility, and it came to a place which was not far from that cedar, and they brought the cedar which had been cast down to it.

7 And I saw that vine opened its mouth and spoke and said to that cedar: Are you not that cedar which was left of the forest of wickedness, and by whose means wickedness persisted, and did evil all those years, and goodness never?

8 And you kept conquering that which was not yours, and to that which was yours you never showed compassion, and you kept extending your power over those who were far from you, and those who ventured near to you held tightly in the toils of your wickedness, and you lifted yourself up always as one that could not be pulled up by the roots!

9 But now your time has sped by and your hour is come. Do you also therefore depart O cedar, after the forest, which departed before you, and become dust with it, and let your ashes be mingled together?

10 And now lay down in anguish and rest in torment till your last time comes, in which you will come again and be tormented still more.

Chapter 37

1 And after these things I saw that cedar burning, and the vine glowing and all around it the plain was full of unfading flowers. And I awoke and arose.

Chapter 38

1 And I prayed and said: O LORD, my Lord, You always enlighten those who are led by understanding.
2 Your law is life, and Your wisdom is right guidance.
3 Make known to me the interpretation of this vision.
4 For You know that my soul has always walked in Your law, and from my earliest days I departed not from Your wisdom.

Chapter 39

1 And He answered and said to me: Baruch, this is the interpretation of the vision which you have seen.
2 As you have seen the great forest which lofty and rugged mountains surrounded, this is the word.
3 The days come, and this kingdom will be destroyed which once destroyed Zion, and it will be subjected to that which comes after it.
4 After a time the kingdom will be destroyed, and another, a third, will arise, and that also will have dominion for its time, and will be destroyed.
5 And after these things a fourth kingdom will arise, whose power will be harsh and evil far beyond those which were before it, and it will rule many times as the forests on the plain, and it will hold firmly for a time, and will exalt itself more than the cedars of Lebanon.

6 And by it the truth will be hidden, and all those who are polluted with sinfulness will flee to it, as evil beasts flee and creep into the forest.

7 And when the time of its end and fall has approached, then the kingdom of My Messiah will be revealed, which is like the fountain and the vine, and when it is revealed it will root out the multitude of its host.

8 And concerning that which you have seen, the lofty cedar, which was left out of that forest, and the fact, that the vine spoke those words with it which you did hear, this is the word.

Chapter 40

1 The last leader of that time will be left alive, when the multitude of his hosts will be put to the sword, and he will be bound, and they will take him up to Mount Zion, and My Messiah will convict him of all his unlawful deeds, and will gather and set before him all the works of his hosts.

2 And afterwards he will put him to death, and protect the rest of My people which will be found in the place which I have chosen.

3 And his kingdom will stand for ever, until the world of corruption is at an end, and until the times aforesaid are fulfilled.

4 This is your vision, and this is its interpretation.

Chapter 41

1 And I answered and said: For whom and for how many will these things be or who will be worthy to live at that time?

2 I will speak to you everything that I think, and I will ask of You regarding those things about which I think.

3 I see many of Your people who have with drawn from Your covenant, and cast from them the yoke of Your law.

4 But I have seen others who have forsaken their vanity, and fled for refuge beneath Your wings.

5 What will become of them or how will the last time receive them?
6 Or perhaps the time of these will certainly be weighed, and as the beam inclines will they be judged accordingly?

Chapter 42

1 And He answered and said to me: "I will show you these things also.
2 To whom will these things be, and how many will they be?"
3 To those who have believed there will be the good which was spoken of before, and to those who despise there will be the contrary.
4 And regarding those who have drawn near (to Me) and those who have withdrawn (from Me) this is the word. As for those who were before subject (to Me), and afterwards withdrew and mingled themselves with the seed of mingled peoples, the time of these was the former, and was accounted as something exalted.
5 As for those who before knew (Me) not but afterwards knew life, and mingled (only) with the seed of the people which had separated itself the time of these (is) the latter, and is accounted as something exalted.
6 Time will succeed to (advance) time and season to season, and one will receive from another, and then with a view to the conclusion everything will be compared according to the measure of the times and the hours of the seasons.
7 Corruption will take those that belong to it, and life will take those that belong to it.
8 And the dust will be called, and there will be said to it: Give back that which is not yours, and raise up all that you have kept until its time.

Chapter 43

1 But, do you, Baruch, direct your heart to that which has been said to you, and understand those things which have been shown to you? For there are many eternal comforts for you.

2 You will leave this place, and you will pass from the regions which you see now, and you will forget whatever is corruptible, and will not again recall those things which happen among mortals.

3 Go and command your people, and come to this place, and afterwards fast seven days, and then I will come to you and speak with you.

Chapter 44

1 And I, Baruch, went from that place and came to my people, and I called my first-born son and the Gedaliahs my friends, and seven of the elders of the people, and I said to them:

2 I go to my fathers according to the way of all the earth.

3 But you should not withdraw from the way of the law, but guard and admonish the people which remain;

4 that they should not withdraw from the commandments of the Mighty One, for you see that He whom we serve is just, and our Creator is no respecter of persons.

5 And see what has happened to Zion, and what has happened to Jerusalem.

6 For the judgment of the Mighty One will be made known, and His ways, which, though past finding out, are right.

7 For if you endure and persevere in fear (respect / awe) of Him, and do not forget His law, the times will change over you for good. And you will see the consolation (reward) of Zion.

8 Because whatever exists now is nothing, but that which will be is very great. For everything that is corruptible will pass away, and everything that dies will depart, and all the present time will be forgotten, nor will there be any remembrance of the present time, which is defiled with evil.

9 That which runs now runs to vanity, and that which prospers will quickly fall and be humiliated.

10 That which is to come will be the object of desire, and for that which comes afterwards will we hope.

11 For it is a time that will not pass, and the hour comes which abides for ever.

12 And the new world (comes) which is blessedness and does not turn to corruption for those who depart to it, but it has no mercy on those who depart to torment, and it leads to perdition those who live in it.

13 For these are they who will inherit that time which has been spoken of, and theirs is the inheritance of the promised time.

14 These are they who have acquired for themselves treasures of wisdom, and with them are found stores of understanding, and they have not withdrawn from mercy and the truth of the law have they preserved.

15 For to them will be given the world to come, but the dwelling of the rest, who are many, will be in the fire."

Chapter 45

1 Instruct the people as far as you are able, for that labor is ours. For if you teach them, you will quicken them.

Chapter 46

1 And my son and the elders of the people answered and said to me: Has the Mighty One humiliated us to such a degree as to take you from us quickly?

2 We will truly be in darkness, and there will be no light to the people who are left For where again will we seek the law, or who will distinguish for us between death and life?

3 And I said to them: I cannot resist the throne of the Mighty One; nevertheless, there will not be wanting in Israel for a wise man, nor a son of the law to the race of Jacob.

4 But only prepare your hearts, that you may obey the law, and be subject to those who in fear are wise and understanding;

5 And prepare your souls that you may not leave them.

6 For if you do these things, good things will come to you., which I before told you of; nor will you fall into the torment, of which I testified to you before.

7 But with regard to the word that I was to be taken I did not make it known to them or to my son.

Chapter 47

1 And when I had gone out and dismissed them, I went from there and said to them:

2 I go to Hebron: for that is where the Mighty One has sent me. And I came to that place where the word had been spoken to me, and I sat there, and fasted seven days.

Chapter 48

1 And it came to pass after the seventh day, that I prayed before the Mighty One and said, O my Lord, You summon the advent of the times and they stand before You;

2 You cause the power of the ages to pass away, and they do not resist You; You arrange the method (progress / procedures) of the seasons, and they obey You.

3 You alone know the duration of the generations, and You do not reveal Your mysteries to many.

4 You make known the multitude of the fire, and You weigh the lightness of the wind.

5 You explore the limit of the heights, and You scrutinize the depths of the darkness.

6 You care for the number which pass away that they may be preserved and You prepare an habitation (abode) for those that are to be.

7 You remember the beginning which You have made, and the destruction that is to be You do not forget.

8 With nods of fear and indignation You command the flames, and they change into spirits, and with a word You quicken that which was not, and with mighty power You hold that which has not yet come.

9 You instruct created things in the understanding of You, and You make wise the spheres (orbs / heavenly bodies) so as to minister in their orders.

10 Armies innumerable stand before You and minister in their orders quietly at Your nod.

11 Hear Your servant and give ear to my petition.

12 For in a little time are we born, and in a little time do we return.

13 But with You hours are as a time (an age / eon), and days as generations.

14 Be not angry with man; for he is nothing and take not account of our works; for what are we?

15 For by Your gift we come into the world, and we depart not of our own will.

16 For we said not to our parents, Beget us, Nor did we send to Sheol (place of the dead) and say, Receive us.

17 What therefore is our strength that we should bear Your rage or what are we that we should endure Your judgment?

18 Protect us in Your compassions, and in Your mercy help us.

19 Behold the little ones that are subject to You, and save all that draw near to You: Do not destroy the hope of our people, and do not cut short the times (occurrences) of our aid.

20 For this is the nation which You have chosen, and these are the people, to whom You find no equal.

21 But I will speak now before You, and I will say as my heart thinks.

22 In You do we trust, for Your law is with us and we know that we will not fall so long as we keep Your statutes.

23 To all time are we blessed at all events in this that we have not mingled with the Gentiles.

24 For we are all one celebrated people, who have received one law from One:

25 And the law which is among us will aid us, and the surpassing wisdom which is in us will help us.

26 And when I had prayed and said these things, I was greatly weakened. And He answered and said to me: You have prayed simply, O Baruch, and all your words have been heard.

27 But My judgment exacts its own and My law exacts its rights.

28 For from your words I will answer you, and from your prayer I will speak to you.

29 For this is as follows: he that is corrupted is not at all (is as though he does not exist);

30 He has acted sinfully in any way he could and has not remembered my goodness, and has not remembered My goodness, nor accepted My long-suffering.

31 Therefore you will surely be taken up, as I before told you.

32 For that time will arise which brings affliction; for it will come and pass by with quick vehemence, and it will be turbulent coming in the heat of indignation.

33 And it will come to pass in those days that all the inhabitants of the earth will be moved one against another, because they do not know that My judgment has drawn near.

34 For there will not be found many wise at that time, and the intelligent will be but a few. Moreover, even those who know will most of all be silent.

35 And there will be many rumors and tidings, not just a few. And the actions and deeds of spirits (phantoms) will be manifest, and many promises will be recounted. Some of them (will prove) idle, and some of them will be confirmed.

36 And honor will be turned into shame, and strength will be humiliated into contempt, and decency will be destroyed, and beauty will become ugliness.

37 And many will say to many at that time: "Where has the multitude of intelligence hidden itself, and to what place has the multitude of wisdom removed itself?"

38 And while they are thinking on these things, envy will arise in those who had not thought highly of themselves, and passion will seize him that is peaceful, and many will be stirred up in anger to injure many, and they will rouse up armies in order to shed blood, and in the end they will perish together with them.

39 And it will come to pass at the same time, that a change of times will manifestly appear to every man, because in all those times they polluted themselves. and they practiced oppression, and walked every man in his own works, and remembered not the law of the Mighty One.

40 Therefore a fire will consume their thoughts, and in flame will the control of their thoughts be tested; for the Judge will come and will not tarry, because each of the inhabitants of the earth knew when he was transgressing. But because of their pride they did not know My Law.

41 But many will certainly weep over the living more than over the dead.

42 And I answered and said: O Adam, what have you done to all those who are born from you? And what will be said to the first Eve who hearkened to the serpent?

43 For all this multitude are going to corruption, nor is there any numbering of those whom the fire will devour.

44 But again I will speak in Your presence.

45 You, O LORD, my Lord, know what is in Your creature.

46 Long ago You command the dust to produce Adam, and You know the number of those who are born from him, and how far they have sinned before You, who have existed and not confessed You as their Creator.

47 Their end will convict all of them, and Your law which they have transgressed will reward (revenge) them on Your day.

48 But now let us dismiss the wicked and inquire about the righteous.

49 And I will recount their blessedness and not be silent in celebrating their glory, which is reserved for them.

50 This transitory world which you live, has made you endured much labor in a short time, so in that world to which there is no end you will receive great light.

Chapter 49

1 Nevertheless, I will again ask mercy from You, O Mighty One, who made all things.

2 In what shape will those live who live in Your day? Or how will the splendor of those who are after that time continue?

3 Will they then resume this form of the present, and put on these members which hold us back, impeded us, and are now involved in evils, and in which evils are consummated, or will You possibly change these things which have been in the world as You also change the world?

Chapter 50

1 And He answered and said to me: "Hear, Baruch, this word, and write the remembrance of all that you will learn in your heart.

2 The earth will certainly return the dead, which it now receives in order to preserve them. It will not change their form, but it will return them in the same form it received them, and as I delivered them to it, so will it raise them.

3 Then it will be necessary to show the living that the dead have come to life again, and that those who had departed have returned again.

4 And when they have recognized those whom they now know, then judgment will grow strong, and those things which were spoken of prior will come to be.

Chapter 51

1 When that appointed day has passed, the appearance of those who are condemned will be changed and the glory of those who are justified will be shown.

2 For the appearance of those who act wickedly will become worse because they will suffer torment.

3 But the glory of those who have now been justified in My law, who have had understanding in their life, and who have planted the root of wisdom in their heart, their splendor for their face will be changed and glorified. Their face will be turned into the light of their beauty, that they may be able to take and receive the world which does not die, which is promised to them at that time.

4 Those that rejected My law, and stopped their ears that they might not hear wisdom or receive understanding will lament their actions over and above all things.

5 When they see those they were exalted over but who will be exalted and glorified more than they, they will both be transformed, the latter into the splendor of angels, and the former will waste away more as they wonder at the visions when they see the angelic forms.

6 For they will first see these things and afterwards depart to be tormented.

7 But those who have been saved by their works, and to whom the law has been a hope and understanding, and an expectation, and wisdom, and a confidence, will have wonders appear in their time.

8 For they will behold the world which is now invisible to them, and they will behold the time which is now hidden from them:

9 And time will no longer cause them to age.

10 For they will dwell in the high places of that world and they will be made like the angels and they will be made equal to the stars, and they will be changed into every form they desire from beauty to loveliness and from light to glorious splendor.

11 Before them the borders of Paradise will be spread out, and the beauty and majesty of the living creatures which are beneath the throne will be shown to them. They will see the armies of the angels who are held fast by My word, lest they should appear and are held fast by a command, that they may stand in their places until the time of their appearance comes.

12 There will be righteous excellence surpassing that of the angels.

13 For the first will receive the last. Those who have passed away will receive whom they were expecting. Those who had passed away and who we had head of we should expect to see.

14 For they have been delivered from the tribulation of this world and laid down their burden of anguish.

15 For what have men lost their life, and for what have those who were on the earth exchanged their soul?

16 They did not choose the time which is beyond the reach of anguish. But they chose that time whose results are full of lamentations and evils, and they denied the world which does make those who come to it grow old, but they rejected the time of glory. Thus that they will not have the honor of which I told you before."

Chapter 52

1 And I asked: How can we forget those whom are destined for sorrow?

2 Why do we mourn for those who die? Why do we weep for those who depart to Sheol?

3 Lamentations should be reserved for the beginning of the torment to come. Let tears be stored up for the time of destruction.

4 But even in the face of these things will I speak. What will the righteous do now?

5 Rejoice in the suffering which you now suffer. Why do you look for the decline of your enemies?

6 Make your soul ready for what is reserved for you, and prepare your souls for the reward which is stored up for you.

Chapter 53

1 And when I had said these things I fell asleep and I saw a vision. A cloud was ascending from a very large sea, and I kept looking at it and I saw it was full of black and white waters, and there were many colors in those same waters, and it looked like powerful lightning as seen from a summit.

2 And I saw the cloud passing quickly in short courses, and it covered all the earth.

3 Then, after these things that cloud began to pour all the waters that were in it upon the earth.

4 And I saw that all the waters which fell from it looked different.

5 To begin with, the waters were black and there was a lot for a time, and afterwards I saw that the waters became bright, but they were not as much, and after that I again saw black waters, and after these things again bright, and again black and again bright how this was done twelve times, but the black were always more numerous than the bright.

6 At the end of the cloud it rained black waters, and they were darker than had been all those waters that were before, and fire was mingled with them, and where those waters descended, they work devastation and destruction.

7 And after all of this I saw that lightning I had seen on the summit of the cloud seized hold of it and hurled it to the earth.

8 Now that lightning shone very brightly so that it illuminated the whole earth, and it healed those regions where the last waters had descended and work devastation.

9 And it took hold of the whole earth, and had dominion over it.

10 After these things I saw the twelve rivers were ascending from the sea, and they began to surround that lightning and to become subject to it.

11 And because of my fear I awoke.

Chapter 54

1 And I besought the Mighty One, and said: You alone, O Lord, know the deep things of the world before they happen. The things which occur in their times You bring about by Your word. You speed the beginning of these times against the works of the inhabitants of the earth, and the end of the seasons You alone know.

2 For You nothing is too hard. You do everything easily by a nod.

3 You, to whom the depths come as the heights, and whose word the beginnings of the ages serve;

4 You, who reveal to those who fear what You prepared for them so that they may be comforted.

5 You show great acts to those who do not know You. You break down the walls of those who are ignorant, and You light up what is dark, and You reveal what is hidden to the pure, who have submitted themselves to You and in Your law.

6 You have shown your servant this vision. Reveal its interpretation to me.

7 I know that for those things I have asked You about, I have received and answer. You have revealed to me with what voice I should praise You, and with what members of mine I should praises You and cause hallelujahs to ascend to You.

8 If my members were mouths and the hairs of my head were voices, I could not give you adequate food of praise, nor could I worship you as is befitting. I could never tell the glory of your beauty or praise you enough.

9 For what am I among men? Why am I counted among those who are more excellent than I that I have heard all these marvelous things from the Most High and numberless promises from Him who created me?

10 Blessed be my mother among those that bear, and let she that bare me be praised among women.

11 For I will not be silent in praising the Mighty One, and with the voice of praise I will tell His marvelous deeds.

12 For who does deeds like Your marvelous deeds, O God? Who comprehends Your deep thought of life.

13 With Your counsel You govern all the creatures which Your right hand has created. You have established every fountain of light beside You, and You have prepared the treasures of wisdom beneath Your throne.

14 Those who do not love your law perish justly. The torment of judgment awaits those who have not submitted themselves to Your power.

15 For though Adam first sinned and untimely brought death upon all, yet each of those who were born from him has prepared his own soul for the

torment to come, and each one of them has chosen for himself glories to come.

16 It is certain that he who believes will receive reward.

17 But now, you wicked are bond for destruction because you will quickly be visited because you have rejected the understanding of the Most High.

18 His works have not taught you, and you have not been convinced by the skill of His creation which argued with you continually.

19 Adam is therefore not the cause, except for only his own soul, but each of us has been the Adam (man) of his own soul.

20 But You, O Lord, explain (open) to me those things which You have revealed to me, and inform me regarding that which I besought You.

21 For at the creation and until the end of the world, vengeance will be taken upon those who have done wickedness according to the wickedness in them, and You will glorify the faithful according to their faithfulness.

22 For those who are among Your own You rule, and those who sin You blot out from among Your own.

Chapter 55

1 Then, when I had finished speaking the words of this prayer I sat there under a tree that I might rest in the shade of the branches.

2 And I wondered and was amazed as I pondered the multitude of goodness which sinners who are upon the earth have rejected, and the tremendous torment they have hated, though they knew that they would be tormented because of the sin they had committed.

3 And when I was thought about these things the angel Ramiel, who presides over visions of truth, was sent to me, and he said to me:

4 Why does your heart trouble you, Baruch, and why do you have disturbing thoughts?

5 If the report you have only heard regarding judgment moved you so much what will you do when you see it manifest before yours eyes?

6 And if you expect the day of the Mighty One and you are so overcome just by the expectation, what will you do when you come to its actual occurrence?

7 If at the mention of the announcement of the torment of those who have done foolishly, you are so completely upset, how much more will you be when the event reveals astonishing things? And if you have heard announcements of the good and evil things which are coming and are grieved, what will you do when you behold the majesty that will be revealed, which will convict some and cause others to rejoice.

Chapter 56

1 Nevertheless, because you have asked the Most High to reveal to you the interpretation of the vision you have seen, I have been sent to tell you.

2 And the Mighty One has certainly made known to you the arrangement of the times which have passed, and are destined to pass in His world regarding those of deceit and of those of truth from the beginning of its creation to its end.

3 As you saw, a tremendous cloud ascended from the sea, and covered the earth. This is the duration of the world which the Mighty One made when he thought to make the world.

4 And when the world came into being and had left His presence (area of the throne), the time of the world was short, and was established according to the vast intelligence of Him who sent it.

5 And as you saw before on the summit of the cloud, black waters descended previously on the earth. This is the transgression that Adam the first man committed.

6 For since the time he transgressed, (early) untimely death came. Grief was named and anguish was prepared, pain was created, and trouble was born, disease took hold, and Sheol kept demanding to be renewed in blood The birth of children was brought about, and the passion of parents was its fruit, and the greatness of humanity was humiliated, and goodness died.

7 What can be blacker or darker than these things?

8 This is the beginning of the black waters which you have seen.

9 From these black waters, black was derived, and from the darkness, darkness was produced.

10 For he became a danger to his own soul and even to the angels.

11 At the time when he was created, they (the angels) enjoyed liberty.

12 But some of them descended, and mingled with the women.

13 And those who did so were tormented in chains.

14 But the rest of the multitude of the angels, of which there is no number, restrained themselves.

15 Those who lived on the earth perished together with them (the fallen angels) through the waters of the flood.

16 These are the first black waters.

Chapter 57

1 And after these waters you saw bright waters. This is the spring of Abraham and his generations and the birth of his son and his son's son and of those like them.

2 Because at that time the unwritten law was named among them. The words of the commandments were then fulfilled. Belief in the coming judgment was then born and hope of the world that was to be renewed was then created. The promise of life to come was began.

3 These are the bright waters, which you have seen.

Chapter 58

1 The third black waters you have seen are the mingling of all sins, which the nations committed after the death of those righteous men in the wickedness of the land of Egypt where they did unrighteousness. And they made their sons serve unrighteousness.

2 However, these also perished in the end.

Chapter 59

1 And the fourth bright waters you have seen are the birth of Moses, Aaron, Miriam, and Joshua the sons of Nun and Caleb and of all those like them.

2 For at that time the lamp of the eternal law shone on all those who sat in darkness, which announced to them that believe the promise of their reward, and to them that deny, the torment of fire which is reserved for them.

3 But also the heavens at that time were shaken from their place, and those who were under the throne of the Mighty One were disturbed, when He was taking Moses to Himself For He showed him many reproofs along with the principles of the law and the completion of the times, as He also showed to you. He also showed the pattern of Zion and its size, in the pattern of which the sanctuary of the present time was to be made.

4 But then also He showed him the size of the fire, the depths of the abyss, the weight of the winds, the number of the drops of rain,

5 How much of (His) anger (He) holds back, and the amount of long-suffering (He has), and the truth of (His) judgment,

6 And the origin of wisdom, the wealth of understanding, the wellspring of knowledge,

7 The height of the air, and the greatness of Paradise, the end of the ages, and the beginning of the day of judgment,

8 The amount of the offerings, the earths which are yet to come,

9 The mouth of Gehenna (hell), the place of vengeance, the place of faith, and the place of hope,

10 The visions of future torment, the multitude of angelic hosts, the flaming hosts, the splendor of the lightning and the voice of the thunders, the orders of the captains of the angels, the treasuries of light, and the changing of times, and the searching of the law.

11 These are the bright fourth waters which you have seen.

Chapter 60

1 The fifth black waters you have seen raining are the deeds the Amorites committed, and the spells of their incantations which they performed, and the unrighteousness contained in their mysteries, and the pollutions they mixed.

2 Even Israel was polluted by sins in the days of the judges, though they saw many slip from Him who made them.

Chapter 61

1 And the sixth bright waters you saw is the time in which David and Solomon were born.

2 That was the time of the building of Zion, the dedication of the sanctuary, the shedding of much blood of the nations that sinned, and many offerings which were given in the dedication of the sanctuary.

3 Peace and tranquility existed at that time, And wisdom was heard in the congregation.

4 The wealth of understanding was magnified in the congregations, and the holy feasts and ceremonies were carried out in blessings and great joy.

5 The judgment of the rulers was without guile and it was witnessed as such. The righteous law of the Mighty One was accomplished with truth.

6 And the land was then loved by the Lord because its inhabitants sinned not and it was glorified beyond all lands. At that time the city Zion ruled over all lands and regions.

7 These are the bright waters which you have seen.

Chapter 62

1 And the seventh black waters which you have seen is the perversion brought about by the counsel of Jeroboam, who decided to make two calves of gold:

2 And all the iniquities which kings who were after him sinfully worked,

3 And the curse of Jezebel and the worship of idols which Israel practiced at that time.

4 The withholding of rain, and the famines which occurred until women ate the fruit of their wombs,

5 And the time of their captivity which came upon the nine tribes and a half tribe because they were in many sins.

6 Then, Salmanasar, King of Assyria, came and led them away captive.

7 But regarding the Gentiles, how they always were sinful and wicked, and always unrighteousness would be wearisome to tell

8 These are the seventh black waters which you have seen.

Chapter 63

1 And the eighth bright waters you have seen is the correction and uprightness of Hezekiah King of Judah and the grace of God which came upon him.

2 When Sennacherib was aggressing in order to kill Hezekiah the deadly rage of Sennacherib troubled Hezekiah because a great population of the nations were with him .

3 When Hezekiah the king heard those things which the king of Assyria was devising and how he planned to come and seize him and destroy his people, the two and a half tribes which remained and how he wished to overthrow Zion Hezekiah trusted in his works, and had hope in his righteousness, and spoke with the Mighty One and said:

4 "Look! Sennacherib is prepared to destroy us, and he will boast and strut when he has destroyed Zion."

5 And the Mighty One heard him because Hezekiah was wise and so He listened to his prayer because he was righteous.

6 Then the Mighty One commanded Ramiel, His angel, who speaks with you.

7 And I went out and destroyed their population, whose count of their chiefs alone was a hundred and eighty-five thousand, and each one of them had an equal number that he commanded.

8 And at that time I burned their bodies from the inside out, but their clothing and weapons I preserved outwardly so that more wonderful deeds of the Mighty One might be seen, and that because of this His name might be spoken of throughout the whole earth.

9 And Zion was saved and Jerusalem delivered and Israel was freed from tribulation.

10 And all those who were in the holy land rejoiced, and the name of the Mighty One was mentioned and glorified.

11 These are the bright waters which you have seen.

Chapter 64

1 "The ninth black waters which you saw was all the wickedness which was in the days of Manasseh the son of Hezekiah.

2 His deed showed that he had no regard for God. He killed the righteous people, and he forcibly stole away judgment. He shed the blood of the

innocent. He violently raped women, he overturned the altars and destroyed their offerings. He drove out their priests so that they could not minister in the sanctuary.

3 He made an image with five faces: four of them looked to the four winds, and the fifth on the top of the image was a passionate enemy of the Mighty One.

4 Then rage went out from the presence of the Mighty One to the intent that Zion should be pulled up by its roots, just like it happened in your days.

5 A decree went out from God against the two tribes and a half tribe that they should also be led away captive, as you have now seen.

6 The impiety of Manasseh increased greatly to the point that it removed the praise of the Most High from the sanctuary.

7 Because of this Manasseh was then named "the impious", and finally his dwelling was in the fire.

8 For though his prayer was heard by the Most High, finally, when he was thrown into the brass horse and the brass horse was then melted, it was meant as a sign to him for that time.

9 He had not lived perfectly. He was not worthy but this was done so that he might know by whom he should be tormented in the end.

10 For He who is able to reward is also able to torment.

Chapter 65

1 Manasseh acted without regard for God, and thought that in his time the Mighty One would not look into these things.

2 These are the ninth black waters which you saw.

Chapter 66

1 "And the tenth bright waters which you have seen is the purity of the generations of Josiah King of Judah, who was the only one at the time who submitted himself to the Mighty One with all his heart and with all his soul.

2 He cleansed the land from idols, and sanctified all the vessels which had been polluted, and restored the offerings to the altar, and the horn of the holy was lifted, and he exalted the righteous, and honored all that were wise in understanding, and brought back the priests to their ministry, and destroyed and removed the magicians and enchanters and necromancers from the land.

3 He killed the sinners that were living and they also took from the sepulchers the bones of the dead and burned them with fire.

4 He established the festivals and the Sabbaths in their sanctity. He burned their polluted ones in the fire and the lying prophets which deceived the people were also burned in the fire, and the people who listened to them when they were living, he threw them into the brook Cedron, and heaped stones upon them.

5 And he was zealous with passion for the Mighty One with all his soul. He alone was steadfast in the law at that time, so that he left none that was uncircumcised, or that sinned in all the land, all the days of his life.

6 Therefore he will receive an eternal reward, and he will be glorified with the Mighty One beyond many at a later time.

7 For on his account and on account of those who are like him were the honorable glories, of which you was told before, created and prepared.

8 These are the bright waters which you have seen.

Chapter 67

1 "And the eleventh black waters which you have seen is the calamity which is now befalling Zion.

2 Do you think that there is no anguish to the angels in the presence of the Mighty One because Zion was delivered up in such a way or that the Gentiles boast in their hearts, and amass before their idols? The gentiles say, 'she who so often trod down is now trodden down and she who reduced others to slavery is now a slave herself.

3 Do you think that in these things the Most High rejoices, or that His name is glorified?

4 But how will it effect His righteous judgment?

5 Yet after these things the gentile will seize and scatter them in the tribulation and they will dwell in shame in every place.

6 Because Zion is delivered up and Jerusalem has been laid waste, idols prosper in the cities of the Gentiles, and the cloud of smoke from the incense of the righteousness which the commands is now extinguished in Zion. In every place in and surrounding Zion there is the smoke of sin.

7 The King of Babylon who has now destroyed Zion will arise, and he will boast about being ruler over the people, and he will speak great things in his heart in the presence of the Most High.

8 But he will fall in the end. These are the black waters.

Chapter 68

1 The twelfth bright waters which you have seen is the word.

2 After these things occur a time will come when your people will fall into distress, so that they will all run the risk of perishing together.

3 Nevertheless, they will be saved, and their enemies will fall in their presence.

4 In time they will have much joy.

5 After a little space of time Zion will be built again, and its offerings will be restored again, and the priests will return to their ministry, and the Gentiles will come to glorify it, but not as fully as they did in the beginning.

6 After these things there will be the fall of many nations.

8 These are the bright waters which you have seen."

Chapter 69

1 The last waters which you have seen were darker than all that were before them. Those were after the twelfth number were collected together. They belong to the entire world.

2 The Most High made division from the beginning, because He alone knows what will happen due to the depth and breadth of the sin which will be committed before Him. He foresaw six kinds of them.

5 He also foresaw six kinds of good works of the righteous which will be accomplished before Him. They will go beyond those which He will work at the end and conclusion of the age.

6 For Him there were not black waters with black, nor bright with bright; because it is the end.

Chapter 70

1 Hear the interpretation of the last black waters which are to come after the all other black waters. This is the word.

2 The days will come when the time of the age is ripe that is the harvest of evil and good seeds. This is what the Mighty One will bring upon the earth and its inhabitants and upon its rulers. It is disturbing to the spirit and lethargy of heart.

3 They will hate one another, and provoke one another to fight, and the cruel will rule over the honorable, and those of low status will be honored above the famous.

4 Many will be delivered into the hands of the few, and those who were nothing will rule over the strong. The poor will have abundance beyond the rich, and the wicked will exalt themselves above the heroic.

5 The wise will be silent, and the foolish will speak. The ideas of men will not be heeded, nor will the counsel of the mighty. The hope of those who hope be will not be rewarded.

6 And when those things which were predicted have come to pass confusion will fall upon all men. Some of them will fall in battle, some of them will die in torment and pain, and some of them will be destroyed by their own people.

7 Then the Most High will reveal those peoples whom He has prepared from before and they will come and make war with the leaders that will be left.

8 And whosoever survives the war will die in the earthquake, and whosoever survives the earthquake will be burned by the fire, and whosoever survives the fire will be destroyed by famine.

9 But whosoever of the victors and the vanquished survives and escapes all these things mentioned before will be delivered into the hands of My servant Messiah.

10 For all the earth will devour its inhabitants.

Chapter 71

1 And the holy land will have mercy on its own, and it will protect its inhabitants at that time.

2 This is the vision you have seen and this is the interpretation.

3 I have come to tell you these things because your prayer has been heard by the Most High.

Chapter 72

1 Listen, regarding the bright lightning which is to come at the end, after the black waters. This is the word.

2 After the signs which you were told of before, when the nations become turbulent, and the time of My Messiah is come, he will summon all the nations. Some of them he will spare, and some of them he will kill.

3 These things will come upon the nations which are spared by Him.

4 Every nation which does not know Israel and has not trodden down the seed of Jacob will be spared.

5 This is because some out of every nation will be subjected to your people.

6 But all those who have ruled over you or have known you will be given up to the sword.

Chapter 73

1 When He has brought everything that is in the world low and has sat down on the throne of His kingdom in peace for the dispensation, joy will be revealed and rest will appear.

2 Healing will descend in the dew and disease will go away and anxiety, pain and sorrow will vanish from among men. Gladness will go forth through the whole earth.

3 And no one will again die before his time (young) nor will adversity suddenly befall any.

4 Judgments, reproach, arguments, revenge, spilling of blood, passions, envy, hatred, and things like these will be condemned when they are removed.

5 For it is these very things which have filled this world with evils. On account of these the life of man has been greatly troubled.
6 Wild beasts will come from the forest and minister to men, asps and dragons (serpents) will come out from their holes to submit themselves to a little child.
7 Women will no longer then have pain when they bear children or suffer torment when they yield the fruit of the womb.

Chapter 74

1 In those days the reapers will not grow weary, nor those that build be weary from work. The works will quicken itself and speed those who doe the work and give them much tranquility.
2 That which is corruptible will be destroyed. It is the beginning of that which is not corruptible.
3 Those things predicted will belong to this age. It is far removed from evil and near to things eternal.
4 This is the bright lightning which came after the last dark waters."

Chapter 75

1 And I asked: Lord, Who can understand Your goodness? For it is incomprehensible.
2 Who can look into your compassions, which are infinite?
3 Who can understand Your intelligence?
4 Who is able to explain the thoughts of Your mind?
5 Who of those born can hope to attain those things unless to him are merciful and gracious?
6 Certainly if You did not have compassion on those who are under Your right hand they could not come to those things. Only those who are in the numbers you named can be called.

7 We who exist know why we have come and so we submit ourselves to Him who brought us out of Egypt. We will come again and remember those things which have passed. We will rejoice in what has been.

8 But if we do not know why we have come and if we do not recognize the kingdom of Him who brought us up out of Egypt, we will have to come again and seek after those things which have been now. We will be grieved with pain again because of those things which have befallen.

Chapter 76

1 And He answered and said to me: This vision has been revealed and interpreted to you as you asked me to do, now hear the word of the Most High that you may know what is to befall you after these things.

2 You will surely leave this earth, but not by death, but you will be preserved until the end of the age (times).

3 Go up to the top of that mountain, and all the regions of that land, and the figure of the inhabited world, and the tops of the mountains, and the depth of the valleys, and the depths of the seas, and the number of the rivers will pass before you so that you may see what you are leaving, and to what place you are going. Now this will happen after forty days.

4 Go now during these days and teach the people as much as you are able so that they may learn and not die at the last age but they may learn in order that they may live at the last age."

Chapter 77

1 And I, Baruch, went from there and came to the people, and assembled them together from the greatest to the least, and said to them:

2 Hear, children of Israel! See how many of you are who remain of the twelve tribes of Israel.

3 To you and to your fathers the Lord gave a law more excellent than to all peoples.

4 Because your brethren transgressed the commandments of the Most High, He brought vengeance upon you and upon them. He did not spare the former, and the latter also He gave into slavery.

5 He did not leave a trace of them. But you are here with me.!

6 If you direct your ways correctly you will not depart as your brethren departed, but they will come back to you.

7 You worship He who is full of mercy. Your hope is in Him who is gracious and true. He will do good and not evil.

8 Have you not seen what has befallen Zion?

9 Do you think that the place (area/location) had sinned and that is why it was overthrown? Did you think that the land had performed foolishness and that because of this it was delivered up?

10 Don't you know it was because of you who sinned, that those things which did not sin were overthrown? It was because of you who performed wickedness that those thing which did not do foolish acts were delivered up to its enemies?

11 All the people answered and said to me, We can recall the good things which the Mighty One has done for (to) us. We do recall them. There are these things and those things which we do not remember that He in His mercy knows.

12 In spite of this, please do this for us, your people, write to our brethren in Babylon an letter of (religious) teaching and a scroll containing hope so that you may confirm them before you leave us.

13 The religious leaders (shepherds) of Israel have died, and the lamps which gave light are extinguished, and the fountains from which we drank have withheld their stream.

14 We are left in the darkness among the trees of the forest, the thirst of the wilderness."

15 And I answered and said to them: Shepherds and lamps and fountains come from the law: And though we leave, yet the law remains.

16 If you have respect for the law, and are determined to become wise, a lamp will not be lacking, and a shepherd (religious leader) will not fail, and a fountain will not dry up.

17 I will write also to your brethren in Babylon, and I will send by means of men, and I will write in like manner to the nine tribes and a half, and send by means of a bird.

18 And on twenty-first day in the eighth month that I, Baruch, came and sat down under the oak under the shadow of the branches, and no man was with me, but I was alone.

19 And I wrote these two letters; one I sent by an eagle to the nine and a half tribes;

20 And the other I sent to those that were at Babylon by means of three men.

21 And I called the eagle and spoke these words to it: The Most High has made you that you should be higher than all birds.

22 Now go and do not stop in any place, nor enter a nest, nor settle upon any tree, till you have passed over the breadth of the many waters of the river Euphrates, and have gone to the people that dwell there, and drop down to them this letter.

23 Remember that at the time of the deluge Noah received the fruit of the olive from a dove when he sent it out from the ark.

24 The ravens also ministered to Elijah, bringing him food as they had been commanded.

25 Solomon, in the time of his kingdom, when he wished to send or seek for anything, commanded a bird to go out and it obeyed him as he commanded it.

26 So do not tire, and do not turn to the right hand nor the left, but fly and go by a direct way, that you may preserve the command of the Mighty One, according as I said to you.

Chapter 78

1 These are the words of that letter which Baruch the son of Neriah sent to the nine and a half tribes, which were across the river Euphrates, in which these things were written.

2 Baruch the son of Neriah says to the brethren carried into captivity: "Mercy and peace."

3 I bear in mind, my brethren, the love of Him who created us, who loved us from ancient times, and never hated us, but above all taught us.

4 And truly I know that all of us in the twelve tribes are bound by one bond, inasmuch as we are born from one father.

5 Because of this I have been the more diligent to leave you the words of this letter before I die, so that you may be comforted regarding the evils which have come upon you, and also that you may be grieved regarding the evil that has befallen your brethren; and also that you may justify (understand and accept) His judgment which He has decreed against you that you should be carried away captives. What you have suffered is a sentence disproportionably greater than what you have done. But this was done in order that, at the last times, you may be found worthy of your fathers.

6 So, if you consider that you have now suffered those things for your good, that you may not be condemned and tormented in the end, then you will receive eternal hope. But you must remove from your heart all error and vanity, for it was because of this you departed from here.

7 If you so do these things He will never forget you. He who gave His promise to those greater than us but on our behalf, that He will never forget or forsake us, but will gather together again those who were dispersed with much mercy.

Chapter 79

1 Now, my brethren, learn first what befell Zion and how Nebuchadnezzar King of Babylon came up against us.
2 For we have sinned against Him who made us, and we have not kept the commandments which he ordered us to keep. Yet he has not chastened us as we deserved.
3 For what befell you we also suffer in a the highest degree, for it happened to us also.

Chapter 80

1 And now, my brethren, I reveal to you that when the enemy had surrounded the city the angels of the Most High were sent, and they collapsed the fortifications of the strong wall and they destroyed the solid iron corners, which could not be pulled up.
2 Nevertheless, they hid all the vessels of the sanctuary, to prevent the enemy from possessing them.
3 And when they had done these things, they delivered to the enemy the collapsed wall, and the plundered house, and the burnt temple, and the people who were overcome because they were delivered up. They did this so the enemy could not boast and say: " In war. by force have we been able to lay waste to the house of the Most High."
4 They also have bound your brethren and led away them to Babylon, and have forced them to live there.
5 But we, being very few, have been left here..

6 This is the tribulation about which I wrote to you.

7 And certainly I know that alleviation of the pain of the inhabitants of Zion consoles you. You knew that they prospered so your consolation was greater than the tribulation which you endured in having to leave it.

Chapter 81

1 But regarding consolation, listen to my word.

2 I was grieving regarding Zion, and I prayed for mercy from the Most High, and I said:

3 How long will these things last for us? Will we always have these evils on us?"

4 The Mighty One acted according out of the multitude of His mercies and according to the vastness of His compassion. He revealed to me His word so that my suffering would be relieved. He showed me visions that I should not again endure anguish. He made known to me the mystery of the times. And the advent of the hours he showed me.

Chapter 82

1 Therefore, my brethren, I have written to you, that you may comfort yourselves regarding the multitude of tribulations.

2 You know that our Maker will certainly avenge us and do to our enemies according to all that they have done to us. The end, which the Most High will make is very near will bring His mercy and the final result of His judgment is by no means far off.

3 For now we see the numerous prosperity of the Gentiles, even though they act sinfully and they are like a vapor.

4 We see their great power, even though they act wickedly, But they will become like a drop (of water).

5 We see the strength of their might, even though they resist the Mighty One every hour. But they will be considered as spittle.

6 We consider the glory of their greatness, though they do not keep the statutes of the Most High. But as smoke will they pass away.

7 And we think about the beauty of theirs gracefulness, even though they give it with pollutions. But as grass that withers will they fade away.

8 And we consider the strength of their cruelty, though they do not remember what it brought or how it ended. But as a wave that passes (through them) they will be broken.

9 And we remark about how the brag about being mighty although they deny that it was God that gave it to them. But they will disappear like a passing cloud.

Chapter 83

1 Most High will certainly speed up His times, and He will bring on His hours.

2 He will judge those who are in His world with certainty, and visit truth on all their hidden works.

3 He will examine the secret thoughts, and those things of all the members of man which they laid up in the secret chambers. He will make them appear in the presence of all with reproof.

4 Allow none of these present things to ascend into your hearts, but above all let us be expectant because that which is promised to us will come.

5 Do not let us look to the delights of the Gentiles now but let us remember what has been promised to us in the end.

6 For the end of the times and of the seasons and whatever is with them will cease together.

7 The conclusion of the age will show the tremendous strength of its ruler, when all things come to judgment.

8 Prepare your hearts for that which you have believed or you will be in bondage in both worlds and you be led away captive here and be tormented there.

9 That which is now or which was, or which will come, is the evil fully evil, nor the good fully good.

10 For all your health of this time are turning into sickness, and all strength of this time is turning into weakness, and all the power of this time is turning into impotence, and the energy of youth is turning into old age and death.

11 Every beauty of gracefulness of this time is becoming faded and hateful, and every prideful kingdom of this time is turning into humiliation and shame, and every praise of the glory of this time is turning into the embarrassment of silence, and every empty bragging insult of this time is turning into a mute ruin.

12 Every delight and joy of this time is turning to worms and decay, and every noise of the proud of this time is turning into dust and lethargy.

13 Every possession of riches of this time is being turned into Sheol (hell) alone, and all the yearning of passion of this time is turning into death, and every lustful desire of this time is turning into judgment with torment.

14 Every trick and craftiness of this time is turning into a proof of the truth. Every sweet ointment of this time is turning into judgment and condemnation, and every love of lying is turning to rudely to the truth.

15 Since all these things are done now does anyone think that they will not be avenged? The consummation of all things will come to the truth.

Chapter 84

1 Because of these things I have revealed to you this while I am still alive. I have said these things that you should learn the things that are excellent, for

the Mighty One has commanded me to instruct you. So I will set before you some of the commandments of His judgment before I die.

2 Do not forget that Moses called heaven and earth to witness against you and said:

3 If you transgress the law you will be dispersed, but if you keep it you will be kept." He also used to say these things to you when you, the twelve tribes, were together in the desert.

4 After his death you threw them away from you and because of this there came upon you what had been predicted.

5 Moses used to tell you tell you what would befall you, and now you see they have befallen you because you have forsaken the law.

6 Now, I also say to you after you have suffered, that if you obey those things which have been said to you, you will receive from the Mighty One whatever has been laid up and waiting for you.

7 Let this letter be for a testimony between me and you so that you may remember the commandments of the Mighty One and that there may be to me a defense in the presence of Him who sent me.

8 And remember the law and Zion, the holy land, your brethren, and the covenant of your fathers. Do not forget the festivals and the sabbaths.

9 Deliver this letter and the traditions of the law to your sons after you, as also your fathers delivered them to you.

10 At all times make requests and pray diligently and unceasingly with your whole heart that the Mighty One may hold nothing against you, and that He may not count the multitude of your sins, but instead remember the rectitude of your fathers.

11 If He doe not judges us according to the multitude of His mercies, woe to all us who are born.

Chapter 85

1 Do you not know that in the past and in the generations of old our fathers had helpers? They were righteous men and holy prophets.

2 We were in our own land and they helped us when we sinned, and they interceded for us with Him who made us, because they trusted in their works, and the Mighty One heard their prayer and forgave us.

3 But now the righteous have been gathered and the prophets have fallen asleep, and we also have gone out from the land, and Zion has been taken from us, and we have nothing now except the Mighty One and His law.

4 If therefore we direct and commit our hearts we will receive everything that we lost, and much better things than we lost by many times.

5 For what we have lost would decay, but what we will receive will not be corruptible.

6 Also, I have written to our brethren to Babylon that to them also I may testify to these very things.

7 Let all those things I said before be always before your eyes, because we are still in the spirit and the power of our liberty.

8 The Most High is long-suffering towards us here, and He has shown us what is to be, and has not concealed from us what will happen in the end.

9 Before judgment takes its own (costs), and truth that which is its due, let us prepare our souls so that we may possess and not be taken as a possession and that we may hope and not be put to shame, and that we may rest with our fathers, and not be tormented with our enemies.

10 For the youth of the world is past, and the strength of the creation already exhausted, and the occurrence of the times is very short because they have already passed by. The pitcher is near to the cistern, and the ship to the port, and the course of the journey nears the city, and life to its conclusion.

11 Prepare your souls, so that when you sail and ascend from the ship you may have rest and not be condemned when you depart.

12 When the Most High will bring about all these things there will not be a place left for repentance, nor a limit to the times or a duration for the hours, or a change of ways, or a place to pray, or a way to send pleas, or to receive knowledge, or give of love. There will be no place of repentance for the soul, nor prayers for offences, nor intercession of the fathers, nor prayer of the prophets, nor help of the righteous.

13 There is the sentence of decay, the way of fire, and the path which leads to Gehenna (place of burning/hell/destruction).

14 There is one law (made) by one. There is one age and an end for all who are in it.

15 Then He will save those whom He can forgive, and at the same time destroy those who are polluted with sins.

Chapter 86

1 When you receive this, my letter, read it in your congregations with care.

2 Meditate on it, and above all do this on the days of your fasts.

3 Keep me in mind by means of this letter, as I also keep you in mind in it, always. Fare you well.

Chapter 87

1 And when I had ended all the words of this letter, and had written it without tiring to its close, that I folded it, and sealed it carefully, and bound it to the neck of the eagle, and dismissed it and sent it.

Conclusion

For thousands of years Israel has awaited the judgment and redemption of The Lord. When the world seemed the most unfair and brutal, hope was held out that the end must be near. The end of days was not a frightening event for the Jews of old. It was to be their greatest age, in which God himself judged all other nations as unworthy and rewarded those Jews who followed their God. Obedience to God was judged on how well one adhered to God's law and commandments.

The belief of divine recompense has echoed through history, changing the ways that both Christian and Jews have viewed their world and their destiny.

Even though the texts presented here are not in our western Christian canon, do not think they have not influenced our faith. The books provide insight into how Jews of the time thought, believed, and acted, but more than that, the texts were circulated and therefore bolstered and broadcast the doctrine and history they contained.

If one ever questioned that non-canonical texts influenced our Bible or our faith, we need to look no further than the famous parallel between the Book of Enoch, written in the second century B.C. and the Book of Jude in the New Testament , written in the first century A.D.

Enoch 1:9 And behold! He comes with ten thousand of His holy ones (saints) to execute judgment on all, and to destroy all the ungodly (wicked); and to convict all flesh of all the works of their ungodliness which they have ungodly committed, and of all the hard things which ungodly sinners have spoken against Him.

Jude 1:14-15 And Enoch also, the seventh from Adam, prophesied of these, saying, Behold, the Lord cometh with ten thousands of his saints, To execute judgment upon all, and to convince all that are ungodly among them of all their ungodly deeds which they have ungodly committed, and of all their hard speeches which ungodly sinners have spoken against him.

Yes, it is true. Documents, doctrine, and points of faith not found in our Bible tremendously influenced what has come to be the Judaism and Christianity we know and practice today.

To learn more about ancient texts that influenced our faith look to the following list:

The Lost Book Of Enoch: A Comprehensive Transliteration,
ISBN: 0974633666

The Gospel of Thomas: A Contemporary Translation
ISBN: 0976823349

Fallen Angels, The Watchers, and the Origins of Evil:
A Problem of Choice
ISBN: 1933580100

Dark Night of the Soul - A Journey to the Heart of God
ISBN: 0974633631

The Gnostic Gospels of Philip, Mary Magdalene, and Thomas:
Inside The Da Vinci Code and Holy Blood, Holy Grail
ISBN: 1933580135

Joseph B. Lumpkin

The Book of Jubilees; The Little Genesis, The Apocalypse of Moses
ISBN: 1933580097

THE BOOK OF JASHER
The J. H. Parry Text in Modern English
ISBN: 1933580143

THE LOST BOOKS OF THE OLD TESTAMENT
ISBN: 1933580119

END of DAYS - The Apocalyptic Writings

Joseph B. Lumpkin

"Apocalypse of Abraham"
Notes and Translations

The Slavonic Pseudepigrapha by Andrei A. Orlov 2006

Box, G.H., and Landsman, J.I., The Apocalypse of Abraham (London, New York: The Macmillan Company, 1918).

Gaster, M., "The Apocalypse of Abraham. From the Roumanian Text, Discovered and Translated" in: M. Gaster, Studies and Texts in Folklore, Magic, Medieval Romance, Hebrew Apocrypha and Samaritan Archeology (London: Maggs Brothers, 1925) (repr. New York, 1971)

James, M.R., The Lost Apocrypha of the Old Testament. The Titles and Fragments (London, 1920)

Pennington, A., "Apocalypse of Abraham" in: The Apocryphal Old Testament (ed. H.F.D. Sparks; Oxford: Clarendon, 1984)

Rubinkiewicz, R., "Apocalypse of Abraham." in The Old Testament Pseudepigrapha: Volume 1. Edited by J.H. Charlesworth. Garden City, New York 1985.

"2 Baruch"
Notes and Translations

On Line Notes by Matthew Ellis

Ken M. Penner, David M. Miller, and Ian W. Scott
Initial Digital Text: Craig A. Evans and David M. Miller

2 Baruch From The Apocrypha and Pseudeipgrapha of the Old Testament by R. H. Charles, vol. II , Oxford Press

Translation from the Syriac by R. H. Charles
The Apocrypha and Pseudepigrapha of the Old Testament in English (Oxford: Oxford University Press, 1913) 2: 481-524 Edited and adapted by George Lyons for the Wesley Center for Applied Theology at Northwest Nazarene University

James H. Charlesworth, "BARUCH, BOOK OF 2 (SYRIAC)," Anchor Bible Dictionary, ed. David Noel Freedman (© 1992)

Joseph B. Lumpkin

"The Apocalypse of Thomas"
Notes and Translations

"The Apocryphal New Testament"
M.R. James-Translation and Notes
Oxford: Clarendon Press, 1924

Notes of Joshua Williams
Northwest Nazarene College,
1995

Secret Saying.The Apocalypse of Thomas
By Jackson Snyder
2006

The Old English Apocalypse of Thomas
trans. Daniel Donoghue and Rebecca Schoff

The Apocryphal New Testament
Elliott, J. K. (Editor), Reader, Department of Theology and Religious Studies, University of Leeds

A Collection of Apocryphal Christian Literature in an English Translation
Publication date 1993 (this edition)
Print ISBN-13: 978-0-19-826182-7

"4 Ezra"
Notes and Translations

J. E. Wright, "Esdras, Books of," in *Dictionary of New Testament Backgrounds*, eds. Craig A. Evans and Stanley Porter (Downers Grove, IL: InterVarsity Press, 2000): 337.

Bidawid, R. J. "4 Esdras." In The Old Testament in Syriac according to the Peshi Version. Vol. 4.3. Leiden: Brill, 1973.

Coggins, R. J. and M. A. Knibb. The First and Second Books of Esdras. The Cambridge Bible Commentary, New English Bible. Cambridge: Cambridge University Press, 1979.

Longenecker, Bruce W. 2 Esdras. Guides to Apocrypha and Pseudepigrapha. Sheffield: Sheffield Academic Press, 1995.

Myers, Jacob M. I and II Esdras. Garden City, N.Y: Doubleday, 1974.

Oesterley, W. O. E. II Esdras (The Ezra Apocalypse). WC. London: Methuen, 1933.

Pseudepigrapha, Apocrypha and Sacred Writings
LDS Church 2007

Bible, King James. 4 Ezra OR 2 Esdras, from The holy Bible, King James version (Apocrypha)
Electronic Text Center, University of Virginia Library

Joseph B. Lumpkin

ABOUT THE AUTHOR

Joseph Lumpkin holds a "Doctor of Ministry" degree from Battlefield Bible Institute. He is the author of a number of books on the subjects of religion and philosophy including the best selling book, *The Lost Book Of Enoch: A Comprehensive Transliteration*, published by Fifth Estate Publishers.

He lives near Birmingham, Alabama where he teaches, lectures, and writes as life allows.

END of DAYS - The Apocalyptic Writings

Joseph B. Lumpkin

www.ingramcontent.com/pod-product-compliance
Lightning Source LLC
Chambersburg PA
CBHW070548170426
43201CB00012B/1756